"GROWN-UPS"

ALSO BY CHERYL MERSER

Honorable Intentions:
The Manners of Courtship in the '80s

"GROWN-UPS"

A Generation in
Search of Adulthood

CHERYL MERSER

G. P. PUTNAM'S SONS   NEW YORK

G. P. Putnam's Sons
Publishers Since 1838
200 Madison Avenue
New York, NY 10016

The author gratefully acknowledges permission from Random
House, Inc., to reprint material from *Where Water Comes Together
with Other Water*, poems by Raymond Carver, copyright
© 1984–85 by Raymond Carver.

Library of Congress Cataloging-in-Publication Data

Merser, Cheryl.
"Grown-ups".

Bibliography: p
Includes index.
1. Adulthood—United States.   2. Baby boom
generation—United States.   3. Maturation
(Psychology)   4. United States—Social conditions—
1960–   .   5. Socialization.   I. Title.
HQ799.97.U5M48   1987   305.2′4   87-10846
ISBN 0-399-13233-3

Typeset by Fisher Composition, Inc.

Printed in the United States of America
1   2   3   4   5   6   7   8   9   10

ACKNOWLEDGMENTS

I'd like first to thank my friend and agent Amanda Urban, whose support for this book began long before there *was* a book; and Neil Nyren, who was unfailingly enthusiastic, patient, and helpful throughout its writing, and well after. I couldn't have asked for a more sympathetic editor. For their thoughtful readings of all or parts of the manuscript, I'd like to thank Maria Matthiessen, Amanda Kyser, Erroll McDonald, Carolyn Reidy, Susanna Porter, Victoria Hughes, Ngaere Macray, Robert Wilson, Christopher Idone, Carol Schneider, Annik LaFarge, Becky Saletan, Malcolm Jones, Jill Krementz, Melanie Fleishman, Christine and Yves Istel, and Leslie Merser. For his help with economics, I am grateful to Pete Peterson and for the title I'm indebted to Nora. I'm especially lucky that my friend Lisa Johnson just happens to work at Putnam—my thanks to her, and to the rest of her colleagues there. Finally, I'd like to thank Jason Epstein for sharing his knowledge and for his considerable editorial advice throughout the research for and writing of this book.

This book is for Jason.

CONTENTS

"What I meant was that when you've lived a little longer you'll see what complex blunderers we all are: how we're struck blind sometimes, and mad sometimes—and then, when our sight and our senses come back, how we have to set to work, and build up, little by little, bit by bit, the precious things we'd smashed to atoms without knowing it. Life's just a perpetual piecing together of broken bits."

—EDITH WHARTON

INTRODUCTION

My favorite time in the publishing company where I used to work was after hours, when, without phones ringing, meetings to attend, emergencies to deal with, and everything else that came up between nine and five, I could finally get some uninterrupted work done. I loved seeing a pile of letters stacked neatly in my "out" box, ready to go the next morning, or finishing some copy I'd been trying to write—a line here and a line there—for days. I'd often stay for hours—you had to sign out of the building after seven, and ring for the service elevator after eight, after the passenger elevators were closed down for the night. My assistant, seeing the work piled up the next morning, would try to guess what time I'd left: "Looks to me like eight-thirty."

I was in good company. There were always a few other young people around who, like me, were willing to put in the extra time it took to get ahead. The office seemed cozy at night, after the "coaches," as we, in our office shorthand, called the people already at the top, had gone home to their families or wherever they went. On these evenings, between working spurts, we'd often gather in one office or another to discuss our work, exchange gossip, or conspire about new businesses we were always going to start pretty soon (but not yet). We were easy among ourselves—some of us had had love affairs with one another, but we usually managed to remain friends after the passion had died down. We also ignored that we were competing for raises and promotions. Our camaraderie was important; we often commented that we were growing up together—and we were. Sometimes when office pressure got to be too much, we'd resort to playing football in the halls. More often we were serious: We were proud of our work.

The cast of late-nighters changed some over the almost nine years I worked there; a few moved on to better jobs or were fired and replaced by others; one of us got married and began leaving the office earlier, though a little regretfully, it seemed to me. One by one, we turned twenty-eight, then thirty. Still, you could always find someone after hours to talk or complain to, or lure out to the Japanese restaurant across the street for a drink after work.

I remember one night in particular, in late winter about three or four years ago, when there was still a little weak sun at the end of an unusually mild day. That night, the office had cleared out early, except for five of us who worked virtuously till seven, then, by tacit agreement, packed up our briefcases, turned off our office lights, and headed for the restaurant, where we ended up staying until after one the next morning.

What was unusual about that night was that none of us had anything else to do. If we had boyfriends or girlfriends at the time, they weren't around. Our married man who usually left the office early had tagged along—his wife was attending an awards banquet in connection with her job at an insurance company; the youngest of us, a woman, was nursing the wounds of a short-lived marriage that had just ended. None of us had made dinner plans for the evening or dates for the movies or whatever, as we usually did. There was a trace of group pathos about us, but we weren't lonely, exactly—we felt instead like an odd little family stranded together somewhere, slightly bored with ourselves and one another but safe and comfortable with the boredom. And as the hours passed and still none of us felt inclined to go home, our conversation turned more intimate than our usual debates over office politics, the merits of this first novel or that best-seller, or what the other publishers were doing.

We talked about our parents, scattered here and there, divorced or down in Florida or, in one case, dead. Two of us, a man who threatened at least once a day to quit "the whole thing," and the divorced woman—by now a close friend whose promotions always came at the same time as mine—confided that they were interviewing for other jobs. Both would leave the company within a few months, one to move to Paris. We argued over a magazine-article-perfect couple we all knew, in a two-career marriage with a byzantine child-care schedule yet with "quality time" left over for each other: Was that having it all? someone asked. We discussed our grand plans for the future—the kinds of houses we dreamed of buying, families we wanted to have, how we'd raise kids, our private ambitions, what we thought would constitute the good life. We tried to put into words the vague longings we all shared to "belong to the world" in substantial ways, to contribute more than just an occasional check to save the whales or starving children. We wanted, we concluded with a hint of late-night melodrama, something beyond a name and two dates to mark our graves.

Finally we packed up to go home, pooled our money to cover the by now substantial check ("I'll pay you back tomorrow"), and hailed various cabs to take us to our five practically identical apartments—five beds (queen-size for the married man), five walls of bookshelves, five stereos, five spider plants, five electric coffee grinders. . . .

I shared a cab uptown with the man about to get the new job, but we were quiet during the ride; talked out, I guess. Mine was the first stop, and as I got out of the cab, my friend—a balding, successful editor whose thirty-fifth birthday we had celebrated in the office with a cake not long before—patted me on the shoulder and said in the pseudo-patronizing way he likes to affect, "Don't worry, my child, we'll all be grown-ups someday."

He's got it wrong, I thought, as I pulled the usual bills and flyers out of my mailbox and rang for the elevator, suddenly exhausted. We *were* grown up, grown-ups with offices to go to, work that mattered, bills to pay, clothes to take to the dry cleaner's, jeans that didn't fit the way they used to. We were grown up, all right; that wasn't the problem.

Instead, what had been on our minds all night was adulthood in a richer sense. Though for all practical purposes we were surely grown-up, we still felt somehow that real adults were in a different category: more certain of their place in the world, wiser, their lives intact in ways we did not yet understand. Married, single, divorced, we were all looking for the balance between too much autonomy and not enough. We wanted to be able to stay out till one in the morning, and, at the same time, we wanted to have reasons why we couldn't. We wanted, I suppose, some of the continuity we remembered from our parents' lives—changing the storm windows to screens every spring, or buying new school shoes and notebooks for the kids in September—but we knew that that life exacted a high price, maybe even higher than the cost of our unencumbered lives. Besides, even if you were willing to pay, how would you get there from here? We were thinking, too, about the world beyond the views from our office windows. We had been so excited as, one by one, we'd been promoted to offices of our own. Now we wondered if that was the way we wanted to watch our lives go by. Or if not, what were the other choices? We were grown-ups, it struck me in the elevator, in search of adulthood.

The cover of Gail Sheehy's hugely successful bestseller *Passages* depicts a staircase, with the *P* in the title as the bottom step; from there the staircase goes up and, with the final *S*, disappears. The letters serve as a baluster, so that the staircase will be safe to climb. The concept behind the design is ingenious, suggesting that achieving adulthood can be as easy as climbing a staircase. I was seduced the moment I heard about the book; I couldn't wait to read it.

Published in 1976, *Passages* builds upon the work of experts who have studied the adult life cycle over the course of this century: Else Frenkel-Brunswick, who began her research in pre–World War II Vienna; and Erik Erikson, probably our most influential expert in psychoanalysis and development, whose still classic *Childhood and Society* was published in 1950, after years of clinical work. Sheehy also acknowledges her debt to Daniel Levinson and Roger Gould, among others, who began their developmental work in the 1960s, Levinson writing exclusively about the male life cycle and Gould exploring the respective stages in the lives of men and women. Sheehy popularized this research through her case studies, charting when and how the "crises" of adult life occur, with the same precision with which childhood experts estimate when a child will walk or talk or first begin to break irreplaceable antiques.

According to Sheehy's staircase, you'll break away from your parents at about age eighteen. If you're a man, you'll choose a career in your twenties and, usually, a partner, and then reassess your partner and career as thirty approaches. If you're a woman, the easy way out after breaking from your parents is to "turn to [your] uterus," to become a mother first thing, though you might try working for a while before settling down. In their early thirties, couples will be buying houses, men working purposefully at their careers, women raising the family; at that age, Sheehy writes, "Men in particular concern themselves with 'making it.'" The "deadline decade," ages thirty-five to forty-

five, is life's halftime, a time, Sheehy says, "of danger
and opportunity," your last chance to get the life you
want together. After a successful all-out mid-life crisis,
"at fifty, there is a new warmth and mellowing." And
then Sheehy's book ends. From there she presumably
turns you over to the gerontologists.

I was twenty-five when *Passages* was published—single, newly arrived at my publishing job (following college, a year of graduate school, and a couple of jobs I'd
hated), living alone in a cozy studio apartment, and
feeling hopeful—all in all, not a bad time to begin
thinking about my "life course."

The problem was that I couldn't find my life anywhere in *Passages*. Pull away from my parents at eighteen? Impossible. They had been going through a
drawn-out divorce then, and setting up their new lives.
Sometimes they were pulling away from me; other
times they were unusually needy.

Off and on, I had had what Sheehy calls the natural
"urge to merge," the longing for marriage characteris-
tic of the trying twenties—but with whom? She writes:
"A woman doesn't have to find an independent form
in her twenties. . . . She can become the maker of
babies and baker of brownies, the carrier of her husband's dream." Oh yeah? Not in my world. I had lived
with someone for a while; should I have made him
babies and brownies? He wouldn't have known what to
do with them—nor would I, not at twenty-five. And
who would want to carry around her husband's dream,
anyway? I was loaded down with enough dreams of my
own, thank you.

As for my men friends, Sheehy agrees with Levinson's idea that the two key relationships for men in

their twenties are a mentor and a significant "loved woman." The idea is that the woman will support and encourage the young man when the mentor is off-duty, at night, I assume, and on weekends. But the men I knew wouldn't have known any women who would be willing to play such a subservient role—not in the late seventies, anyway—and they wouldn't have wanted such a woman. Brownies would have scared them.

Sheehy allows that "singlehood can be a life structure of the twenties, too"; but one example she gives of "singlehood" is a woman who worked as a traveling publicist throughout her twenties, then was pregnant at thirty with twins. What has happened to her career is a mystery for several hundred pages, when she turns up with six kids altogether and vague longings for a part-time job. Mainstream men and women in *Passages* aren't single; they go through the life cycle together as couples, variously in or out of synch with each other.

With every passing birthday or two, I'd turn to the book again, thinking maybe I'd find myself at last. Nope. Not that I was miserable or an outcast, or all that different from many of my friends; they hadn't turned up yet either. I read that the average age for men to divorce was thirty and for women twenty-eight. I read that extramarital affairs were common among people in their late twenties. I read that life is supposed to become "more rational and orderly," more settled, as one reaches one's early thirties. I read about women of thirty-five resenting the fact that they have to depend on men for their allowances. And I read about the havoc an all-out mid-life crisis can cause, and how, if you succeed in resolving it, you'll take action to change your life—maybe divorce, quit a job or (for women) find one, move out of your house, start over. Finally, after umpteen readings, *Passages* began to make sense to me: I realized in amazement that what I was reading, down to the details of the deadline-decade divorce and the subsequent rebirth, was the story of my parents' lives.

Sheehy herself says as much. "Besides age, stage, and gender," she writes, "our personality development is influenced by generation and social change." *By generation and social change.* In other words, the staircase to adulthood needs to be redesigned with each new generation and the particular kind of turmoil that each new generation brings. Sheehy hints, too, at a swelling "tide" of men and women, coming of age and changing the rules governing careers, families, adulthood: men and women without the "baggage" of an earlier era to "unpack." Of these young people, she writes: "We don't know yet where they will come out."

Of course: The forms adulthood took for my parents or their parents or, for that matter, for Gail Sheehy need not be the forms it would take for my friends and me. We were the young people of a new generation and had seen our share, God knows, of social change. Now it made sense why my life wasn't in *Passages:* Gail Sheehy is a writer, not a fortune-teller. How could she possibly have known what kind of world I'd grow up into and thus what kind of adult I'd become? How could Erik Erikson—or anyone else— know? More than a decade after *Passages* was published, my jury is still out.

Considered together, the "tide" of men and women to which Sheehy referred is more often called the postwar or baby-boom generation and includes everyone

born between 1946 and 1964, one-third of the population in this country today. There are approximately 78
million of us. However, to lump everyone born within
these eighteen years into one group is a huge distor-
tion, for there are advantages (and disadvantages) to
having been born early or late in the cycle—in some
ways we're really several generations, not one. And like
any statistical group we're as different from one another as we are alike. If there's one quality we share,
it's that most of us, myself included, are by now a little
tired of being called baby boomers, though it's a label
we'll probably carry with us through our retirement,
well into the next century. This book is about the baby-
boom generation in a particular sense, though; it's
about the influence of "generation and social change"
on adulthood in our time.

I am concerned in this book partly with the obvious
trappings of growing up—identities, careers, marriage,
children, houses, Pontiacs. For Sheehy, these were the
"givens" of growing up, but it doesn't take a genius to
see that for many of us, including my friends from the
office, these trappings are neither obvious nor automatic, the way they seemed to be for my parents and
the other adults I knew when I was growing up. A lot
of us settle into careers, families, or houses later than
men and women did a generation ago, or not at all.
But why? And how does this affect the way we define
adulthood?

How, in other words, can you have a career crisis if
you haven't yet found the right career or even a job?
How can you feel trapped by a mortgage if you can't
afford a house? How can you have a seven-year marital
itch if you're still single by the time you're thirty? How

can you have an all-out mid-life crisis at thirty-five if
you're attending your first Lamaze class? How can you
suffer the empty-nest syndrome if you're childless and
approaching forty? How can you deal with the predictable ups and downs of a marriage if both of you are
working all the time and never see each other? And
most important, if we can't use the benchmarks of another generation to guide us through the life cycle,
what benchmarks will we use instead?

These benchmarks are already taking shape. We're
putting our lives in adult order, though the forms
adulthood is taking for us are neither as consistent nor
as restricted, nor as dependable, as they were even a
generation ago. My friend Joan, for example, spent
her twenty-sixth, then her twenty-seventh year wondering, as she puts it, when her "real life" would begin.
She had lots of friends, a good job—but somehow
needed the stamp of a man to validate herself in her
own eyes. Approaching twenty-eight, she bought herself a condominium, fixed it up, and moved on to a
better job. She's not vague about her real life anymore.
She knows the life she's leading *is* her real life. Not that
her story will end here. But buying the condo was taking a step toward growth, awareness, autonomy, freedom from her preconceived ideas of "real life"—call it
adulthood.

Last December I went to the wedding of a male
friend, with whom I used to have a pact: If neither of
us was married by the time we were fifty, we'd marry
each other. We had both been single all our lives and
he hated it more than I did. "Can you die," he once
asked me, "from eating raw hot dogs?" His adjustment
to marriage has been "so-so, not great," he says. He

misses his own room, the privacy of living alone, to which he had grown accustomed. And "I do things like call my wife 'Honey,' because it fits an idea I have of what marriage is supposed to be like. It doesn't feel real. I'm not unhappy, just detached. We had a dinner party awhile ago and I carved roast chicken, just like a husband. I wondered where the movie cameras were. I felt like an actor."

I'm at the age now that my women friends, and some of my men friends, are, to put it mildly, thinking about kids—whether to have them or not; how to find someone with whom to have them "in time"; what will happen to us (will we shrivel up and be not quite human?) if we don't have them. More passages—fertility doctors, amniocentesis, *in vitro,* sperm banks. And one doesn't simply "have kids" anymore, as a part of the natural course of life's events. There's day care to worry about, and careers to sacrifice, and, if the marriage doesn't work out, custody or visitation rights to juggle. Yet the impulse to nurture goes beyond the decision of whether to have a child or not: At a party recently, I met a gay man, a professor, who brought out pictures to show me—of his goddaughter, the child he'd never have. He told me how clever, loving, and funny she was, and wasn't she beautiful? Never has a father been prouder.

And there is our work, the timeless struggle to find a job that means something, pays something, and doesn't take too much away from the soul. "I'm just like my father—a corporate guy," a friend of mine from Detroit says, in horrified awe. His job takes up all his time, he never sees his family, he's not even sure he's unhappy, and he wonders how he got to this point from protesting the Vietnam War and dropping acid not so long ago. At the other extreme: A publishing friend, a successful magazine editor of thirty, says she would like to take up "knitting and tatting for a while. By a nice hearth. Have Betty Friedan's life—*before The Feminine Mystique.*" More often, I meet people who tell me they're ambitious, but they don't yet know for what.

I'm troubled, too, by a comment a friend made to me over the phone the other day. "You won't like this," she said, "but I finally figured out what being a grown-up is. It's getting used to being lonely." We were talking at the end of the day, and she had called me from her office on the pretext of telling me some good news about her career; her voice was lighthearted, and there was office commotion in the background. Yet she had really called to offer this definition of adulthood; she meant it. "How about getting used to being *alone,* isn't that more what you mean?" I asked, because it was disturbing to me that my friend, a lovely young woman with everything going for her, should feel so lonely. "Well, I mean both," she conceded.

I know what she means; we all do: my married friend carving the chicken, my friends from the office, the guy with the goddaughter, Joan in her condominium. Aside from the outer trappings of being a grown-up, there's the matter of adulthood in the spiritual sense: "belonging to the world," as my friends and I described it that night in the restaurant. Not feeling alone—or refusing to accept that feeling separate is one way of belonging to the world.

The adult, as we'll see, has an awareness that reaches beyond his or her immediate life, into the past, the future, the community, nature, the world. An adult isn't just a bull barging through the china shop of life, buy-ing Ferraris and disc players and Aprica strollers for the kids. He or she doesn't simply take from the world but gives something back in return—acts of kindness, children raised carefully, works of art, choices made honorably, the gift of a life well-lived. The adult is re-sponsible for more than just himself; the adult's influ-ence extends beyond her doorstop.

"It is only the gay and innocent and heartless who can fly," says Wendy in *Peter Pan*. "I'm youth, I'm joy," says Peter. Funny how we as the hope-I-die-be-fore-I-get-old generation promoted this peculiar doc-trine, that youth is joy or that real adults are joyless. This book will argue that there were reasons we needed to be young with such a vengeance—and more urgent reasons now why we need to grow up. And the rewards of adulthood more than compensate for any innocence or joy you might have to give up along the way.

Gail Sheehy's most recent book, about survivors, tells how a couple of years ago she adopted a lovely and wise Cambodian orphan and brought her to America from the internment camp where she had been strug-gling to survive. Sheehy saved the child's life and in the process transformed her own. No one of fifty did such a thing in *Passages*, not during the "mellow" years. Risk, renewal, seeking and offering meaning where you can find it: Her book about a child says more to me about adulthood than my umpteen readings of her earlier book did. To belong to the world, you really have to join it—and to recognize when you're being invited to join.

As Walter Lippmann knew, generations ago, "The

critical phase of human experience is the passage from childhood to maturity; the critical question is whether childish habits and expectations are to persist or to be transformed. We grow older. But it is by no means certain that we shall grow up."

| 1 |

CREDENTIALS

In my first grown-up apartment I had a living room, one bedroom, a kitchen (sort of), a bathroom, two roommates, a cat, and more junk than you can imagine—all at a rent that should have provided housing for a king. I loved it. Well, no. At the time I thought the chaos would drive me crazy; we all felt that way. What I love now is the memory of having taken my first adult steps from that overcrowded little haven. I like to review all that has happened since then, as if I were going back to a favorite book.

Armed with little more than hot-off-the-press liberal arts degrees (I also had a master's, in English), my two roommates and I had come to New York from Michigan with the usual fantasies of making our way in the big city, and at twenty-two, we were starting from square one. We needed a place to live; we needed jobs; we had no other friends in town.

We knew that women a few years older than we had often married right after college or after they had worked perfunctorily for a year or two, and then disappeared into a kitchen somewhere. But that sequence seemed long obsolete to us, or would have, had we thought about it. I don't remember that we ever talked about that life, any more than we talked about heading west in a covered wagon. Feminism (and other social currents, as we'll see) had taken us too far downstream for us to believe that we had chosen a career over husband and family. Married or not, most young women we knew in 1973 went to work, or would sooner or later; it was that simple. And anyway, *choice?* What choice? On top of all our other concerns, at that time none of us even had so much as a boyfriend. We "chose" to make it on our own because that's what people, men and women alike, did; because we were genuinely ambitious; and because what would we do otherwise?

Now that I think about it, what we believed at the time was that nothing was permanent: In no way could the uncertain lives we were living in this cluttered apartment be the lives that we'd end up with. For the moment, our lives were composed of replaceable parts, so to speak. We'd get an apartment, sure, but it would be just for now, not forever. Knowing so few people in New York was a temporary problem; we figured friends would come along in time. Somehow we'd find jobs to tide us over, and in the future, way off— though we didn't talk about the future much—there would be powerhouse careers, knights in shining armor, families, dream houses, pretty things, and happy-ever-afters . . . real life. Adulthood.

Meantime we found our apartment. First things first, though our various parents had to guarantee the lease and lend us money for the security deposit. (Growing up doesn't come cheap, we soon discovered.) The apartment, boxy and undistinguished, was one elevator flight up from a busy cross-street, not far from the Fifty-ninth Street Bridge, and noisy. It was summer and you could hear the roar of the buses and the music from the car radios below. No problem—we were ecstatic. It was a place in New York, and that was the main thing for us. We signed a one-year lease, and a year seemed forever. Surely we'd know more by then. A lot could happen in a year.

We arranged, then rearranged our communal bits of furniture. Should the electrical wire spool "table" be painted red or black, and should it be used as a coffee table or an end table? Should the one and only lamp go in the bedroom or living room? (Bedroom, for reading, but we could move it to the living room if we ever made any friends to have over, and of course there'd be lots of money later for more lamps.) We learned the hard way that the tiny black-and-white TV couldn't go on the bookshelves. The shelves were of the sort that attached to metal spring-poles with brackets, and the cat knocked the whole contraption down once or twice a week. So the spool table had to be put in the corner with the stereo on it, far from the precarious bookshelves, and the TV went in the bedroom.

The bedroom, with its three twin beds that we found in various secondhand stores, required even more imagination. None of the beds could be placed near the window; too much soot from the street came in. That left two walls, and a third with the closet door, but we couldn't very well put a bed in front of our only closet. Plus: By whose bed would the lamp go? Maybe the spool table should go in the bedroom? But then what would the stereo go on? Finally we worked it all out, and you could sort of get into the closet if you opened the door only a little, so as not to squash the cardboard packing box with the lamp and clock radio on it. When everything else was in place, we push-pinned our museum-reproduction posters to the walls.

That accomplished, we sent out for Chinese food and, while we waited for our dinner, settled on various twin beds to collaborate on our résumés and watch a rerun of *Gilligan's Island*. Over the next couple of months, we must have seen every *Gilligan's Island* ever made, as we sat at home night after night on a desert island of our own, waiting for our adult lives to begin.

It occurs to me now that everything had to be just so in that first apartment of ours, because for each of us that apartment was our first stake in a grown-up world we didn't yet know how to negotiate. There we could assure one another that we were smart, really smart, and that the right job would come along any day; but out in the world, going to employment agencies or on job interviews for which we were inevitably over- or under qualified, we weren't so sure. At home we could wear our cutoffs and T-shirts; out in the world we wore unfamiliar dress-up clothes we hoped would impress prospective employers with how responsible we were.

Often we'd venture out to explore New York— Chinatown, the Village, Central Park, the museums; the city was magical, and we'd walk for miles. However,

on bad days the summer street life—happy young couples and groups of people about our own age crowded
around sidewalk café tables, rowdy but sophisticated
and living the spirited life we'd imagined for ourselves—reminded us of how alone we felt, how far we
still had to go to be happy. Many times I simply felt
safer staying at home, pretending that the outside
world I hadn't yet broken into didn't exist. If anyone
were to have asked me who I was or what I did, I
wouldn't have known what to say. If anyone had asked
me where I lived, though—well, there at least was a
question with an answer. I live somewhere, therefore
I am.

There were times when I wondered which I wanted
most: a wonderful job, a flourishing social life, a serious boyfriend. . . . It was painful not to be a part of
things, not knowing if my life would ever fill up with
the things I wanted. (As I saw it, I wasn't greedy; "having it all" would have seemed like enough.) The people
I noticed freeze-framed in the cafés back then seemed
to me to have satisfied all such longings; I had fantasies
about the details of their perfect lives. Now, of course,
having spent time myself in cafés, I'm convinced that
they must have had the same worries I did, that they
were casting about for their lives just as I was casting
about for mine. What I know now, but didn't know
then, is that there are no secrets or shortcuts to growing up.

It's uncanny the way prevailing psychological theories of human development invariably mirror prevailing social trends. In 1953, for example, psychologist
R. J. Havighurst isolated eight "developmental tasks"
that, when completed, would transform the young

adult into a mature adult. The first of these was choosing a marriage partner. Havighurst's other criteria included adjusting to marriage, starting a family, and raising children—criteria that reflect to the letter the social organization of the postwar years, when a percentage of Americans higher than ever before married young and had kids. Had Havighurst or anyone else during those years advised a young person to wait a bit before settling down, to concentrate on establishing his or her identity first, or to consider carefully whether he or she wanted a family or would be a suitable parent— advice that seems so sensible today—he would have been denounced or ignored. After the war, nonconformity was as threatening as, twenty years later, it would be virtuous. And as it happened, Havighurst's criteria for maturity were widely quoted for years—until it became embarrassingly clear that fewer and fewer men and women were following his rules for growing up.

There would be few backers today for a developmental agenda that insisted on marriage as the first and essential step to adulthood; it's no coincidence that recent "scientific" theories match up more closely to the ways we live now. Given the fact that more of us are marrying later, if at all, it's no surprise that in current coming-of-age debates, marriage, at least early marriage, is played down. In *Transformations: Growth and Change in Adult Life,* Roger Gould of UCLA describes the tasks of early adulthood this way: "This is it! No more Linus blanket to cover our fear. . . . We can deny that we are now really responsible for our own lives, try to cede our responsibilities to others and limp ahead half-child and half-adult. But the critical issue of our twenties is that we must build our own lives in the complex, unpredictable, real adult world." Whether we're married or not, the key phrase here is "build our own lives."

Gould allows that we can set up adult shop in a number of ways and presents us with a candy-store variety of "lives" for us to choose from in our various stages of development. For example, his options for those aged twenty-two through twenty-eight include: committing oneself wholeheartedly (or not) to a career; remaining single, living with someone, or marrying; one- or two-career marriages; marriages with (or without) children; and accepting (or not) our new status as adults. In other words, "science" has now come full circle to make room for what he calls "new roles with new rules."

Nevertheless, not even Gould's candy store with all its options *feels* like life the way I remember it during my early adult years. As a general rule, developmental theorists lay out life in a straight line, assuming that any of us is capable of undergoing only one developmental step at a time, as though being single or living in a two-career marriage will explain everything that matters about you or me. Scientifically speaking, that may be true, but that's hardly the way life feels, with all its layers and dimensions. Usually life feels as if it's happening all at once—and sometimes it feels a little slow, the way it felt for me when I was just starting out, with my nose pressed to the glass of other people's lives.

Others I knew in the summer of 1973 were coming of age from different directions; a developmental psychologist would have had trouble funneling us all into a single theory. A close high school friend, for example, decided, however unconsciously, to approach adulthood the way her mother had done; she got married that summer, right out of school as her parents had, and I was a bridesmaid at her garden wedding in Connecticut. Just as my apartment was my first stake in the adult world, her marriage would be hers, she thought. I wondered. Would marriage help her to circumvent all the who-am-I, what-am-I-doing-with-my-life questions that so preoccupied me? Or would it prove as flimsy a shelter as my apartment?

It never occurred to me, at least till after her recent divorce, that we both—my friend with her marriage and I with my fledgling life in a new city—were aiming for the same thing: adulthood. She had believed in what she was doing, as had I. Neither of us had been cutting corners: Later on I'd have to learn to live with a man, and later on she would have to face living alone and making her own way in the world—no doubt a harder task when you're also responsible for a small child, as she is now. At the beginning, however, it was as if she'd tried to reach adulthood from the right, and I from the left, so to speak. Sure, there are stages of adult life—but we don't live our lives in the same "order" that Havighurst felt men and women did in his day.

Another friend, this one from college, headed for adulthood from still another direction: His first stake in the real world was his job. He was a science whiz and, while he was still in school, was offered a job with a chemical company in Maryland. He was from Massachusetts and had gone to school there too. He didn't know a soul in Maryland, but he assumed that he'd meet people through his job, that he could set up his adult life there as easily as anywhere else. When he set out for Maryland, he gave us the address of a motel where he planned to stay until he figured out where he wanted to live. Almost a year later, he was still at the motel.

When I asked him how he was doing, he'd answer by describing the job—great job, he was doing well; he had a future there, he thought. Why was he still living in a motel? On that question he was vague. Oh, you know . . . Much later he admitted that he'd been hanging onto that job for dear life, since he had no other stake in the small one-industry town where all his co-workers—as he described them—left the office right at five to go directly home to their families. There was no room for outsiders. He had little in common with them and he had met nobody else, not even someone with whom to play tennis once a week. His "stake," promising as it was, was not enough upon which to build his life. It wasn't long before he accepted another position, closer to Massachusetts.

The fact that we're no longer living our lives according to a single developmental formula might make matters difficult for psychologists trying to codify us—but would have made perfect sense to the nineteenth-century American philosopher William James. Though deeply concerned with human development and awareness, James saw life not as a science but as an art. He had no formula, but he knew how life feels: "In its widest possible sense," he wrote, "a man's self is the sum total of all that he can call his, not only his body and his psychic powers, but his clothes and his house, his wife and children, his ancestors and friends, his reputation and works, his lands and horses, his yacht and bank-account." If you can forgive the sexism of his time, James's idea of the self is easy to picture. You see a man, a self, at the center of a world of substance and achievement. Surrounding him are the layers of his life, the extensions of his influence and responsibility— or so James believed in the 1890s, when he said that man should aim for a perfect balance between his inner and outer worlds.

Now picture my roommates and me, or, for that matter, most anybody just starting out a century later. With our little apartment and our big dreams, we had only the most modest of inner and outer selves—but then so did my friend at the beginning of her marriage, or my other friend hanging onto his job for dear life, or even James himself, who, a century ago, had had a number of what we'd now call identity crises before he was able to take hold of his own life, before he knew who he was.

What James meant by "psychic powers" in that passage is what he elsewhere calls the "self of selves," the central guiding principle around which the other components of the self cohere. Although we'll always be required to juggle several selves (professional selves, party selves, stronger and weaker selves, the selves we display around our families or close friends), James believed that each of us has one overriding spiritual identity—maybe the self we know when we're alone, or the brave or level-headed self we keep promising to assert "next time" we're treated unfairly.

"The seeker of his truest, strongest, deepest self must review the list carefully, and pick out the [self] on which to stake his salvation," James wrote. Once you've got that, you can begin to discard less desirable selves.

"How pleasant," he imagined, "is the day when we give up striving to be young—or slender!" Or to get to the point where a confident self will predominate over a shy self, or a loving self over one that is fearful, and so on.

There's no proven formula for it, but James believed that it's up to each of us to create his or her own reality, to find the right "self" and assert it. Maybe because we had no choice, my roommates and I must have believed the same thing without even thinking about it: that we could create full lives for ourselves where once there were none, that we could simply *will* these lives into existence.

We had no way of knowing it, but we were building our lives the way Americans (or American men anyway) had been doing it since long before James's time—though with some differences. In one of his essays, James asked, "What are the causes that make communities change from generation to generation?" We would come to understand the differences very well. We were members of the largest generation in our history, and the largest generation of college graduates, all competing for jobs; we were the generation that would test new "definitions" of men and women. As we'll see, there were mixed messages from the sixties to unravel. And many of us felt that, without the props of close families, supportive communities, religions, and traditions to lean upon, we were on our own in ways James couldn't have imagined.

If you take James's definition of the self, set it here and now in your own life, adjust the language to reflect what we might hope for and expect from life today—instead of horses and yachts—you'll have an approximate idea of what I like to think adulthood is all about: It's about the capacity of the evolving self to make successive and successful connections to an unpredictable and changing world.

As we'll see, our world, as opposed to James's, is at the same time both more and less welcoming to fledgling adults. On the down side, many of James's credentials may seem out of reach for nearly all of us. Lands? In James's lifetime, land in this country was so plentiful that every freed slave was promised forty acres and a mule—forty acres! Now, according to one recent estimate, the *average* price of a single-family home (no mule) is about $100,000, and such a house would not be sitting on anything that could remotely be called "lands."

Work? Since the early seventies, when the members of the postwar generation were vying for their first jobs, the number of college graduates has increased by 126 percent, while the economy has wavered between hysterical prosperity and closing up as tight as a clam around your finger. At the same time, our economy has shifted dramatically from producing goods to "producing" services (one example is that there are now more of us who process, prepare, play with, and serve food than there are who raise it, farm it, or fish for it), and has undergone the tumult of accommodating a sharply increasing percentage of female workers. By any fiscal measure, the economy has not been welcoming to young people over the past decade or so. It's shaky out there; more than half the taxi drivers in New York City, for example, have at least two years of college behind them. (On the other hand, the good news is that some forecasters predict that, with this large postwar generation for the most part settled into jobs, and with a smaller cohort coming up behind, the economy might allow more room to maneuver.) As for bank accounts, I wouldn't know. Like too many of us, I plan to do my saving later on.

Families? Children? Often-cited statistics tell part of this story. Nearly a quarter of us in the postwar generation will not marry, and among those of us who do, about half will divorce. One-third of the women born in the 1950s will not have children, and not all by choice. And while it's too early to predict childbearing rates for women born in the 1960s, it's likely that these low-fertility trends will continue: Among women professionals aged eighteen to forty-four, 48 percent are childless, as are 50 percent of those women with four or more years of college behind them.

There is no way to disguise these lonely statistics; they speak for themselves. Still, if we come up short quantitatively—and by now it's widely known that, at least in comparison with our parents' generation, we do—our qualitative expectations are something else again.

Take friendship, for example, another of James's credentials. I would argue that as the nuclear family is less the center of our lives (and where it is, it's not the kind of nuclear family it was in Dick, Jane, and Sally's day), friendship has taken on new meaning in our time. Last Christmas, as I decorated the tree, I remember mourning that I didn't have a child of my own to buy presents for—but then came Christmas Eve, a bunch of friends came over, and the occasion was so lovely and festive that I felt myself among family. At that moment I felt my life was as full and happy as anyone's. I felt lucky.

In the same way, as I hope this book will show, we're

adapting James's other credentials to our possibilities, building our lives as he would have expected us to, given the raw materials of our time. Think of the range of choices we have today, choices that weren't so easy when our parents were young—to be single and still be "okay," to live openly with a lover (of either sex), to delight in our bodies and our extended youth, to enjoy real equal-partner marriages. That we can divorce without shame, tragic as the divorce rate is, is an advance, preferable to living in a miserable marriage; the gains women have made count in our favor. We're comfortable with leisure and travel; and it seems to me that fresh flowers are somehow easier to come by today than when I was young—that counts for a lot. If we're up against limits, as all generations have been, we are also freer to make choices within those limits.

I had no ideas of limits in the summer of 1973, however, or of how many choices I had—or where my psychic powers were, or if I'd ever have a date again, or if I'd get a job in time to pay the rent. Even so, with a determination that I admire more now than I did then, my roommates and I intuited James's message, as we all must, and accepted his challenge. The first step, of course, was the chicken-and-egg question of growing up: How can you keep adding layers to the self when there's no self there to begin with—or more accurately, when the selves that exist are the wrong ones for the world in which you're living? Like anyone else coming of age, my roommates and I had selves (we knew how to be our parents' children and how to be students; we knew a little by then about our feminine and sexual selves; we could mimic setting up a household), but the selves we possessed were those of our childhood, and of little use in the adult world, we found. I can't speak for my friends, but all I knew about myself when I started out was that there was a self of selves in there somewhere, but it's been harder for me to find and hang onto than a contact lens lost in the sea. Though it's easier now, it's still not something I can take for granted.

In time, actually in a very short time, everything changed for my roommates and me. Within weeks, we were putting the energy with which we had "decorated" our apartment into our first jobs. One of our posters disappeared, and one day I saw it pinned to a roommate's bulletin board over her desk. We got a new lamp first thing. Before our lease was up, we found a great new apartment, bigger, with high ceilings and built-in bookcases; the crash-prone shelves were put away. Little by little there were friends, dates. Pretty soon we were living separate lives, going in three directions on Saturday nights. *Gilligan's Island* evenings were rare.

Before long, we no longer lived together at all, and after a while we were closer to other people than we were to each other; we grew apart. That's natural, too, if a sad part of the process. Beryl Markham describes such change in her memoir, *West with the Night:* "Life had a different shape; it had new branches and some of the old branches were dead. It had followed the constant pattern of discard and growth that all lives follow. Things had passed, new things had come."

Which came first for us, the beginnings of our adult selves or our first adult credentials? Hard to say.

Life, with all its good times and disappointments, rarely happens in sequence, but all at once, a credential here, a self emerging there. Slowly, we joined the world, though we were still waiting to be transformed into real adults. Within a few months of one another, we all turned twenty-three, with something to celebrate.

| 2 |

INVENTING ADULTHOOD

There's a shoestore near where I live that sells both men's and women's shoes. When I was browsing in there late one afternoon last fall, after a morning working at my computer, the only other customer was a young man dressed stylishly in jeans and a sweater. He was trying on a pair of conventional black loafers with little gold buckles and looking at his feet in dismay. "Don't you think these shoes look a little old for me?" he asked me, since I was the only one around to ask.

"I don't know; how old are you?" I answered, thinking that I might find something new about adulthood from this young man's attitude about shoes. He was twenty-one, it turned out, and, though I'm sure he thought I was a bit odd, I began trying on shoes myself, one pair after another, in order to keep the conversation going. He had graduated the previous spring from Cornell (a psychology major) and, after spending the summer at his parents' country house on the New Jersey shore, had entered his father's Wall Street business, not at the bottom but somewhere in the middle. (He was still looking at the loafers on his feet in the little floor mirror; I was trying on neon-yellow rain boots.)

Having moved over to the full-length mirror to study the whole effect, he returned to say that he had an office with windows, but it wasn't clear to him exactly what he was supposed to be doing in it. He didn't seem very happy about the "job," though he was impressed by the office itself, with its view of New York Harbor and the Statue of Liberty, and he liked having a secretary, even if he had to "share" her with two of his colleagues. What seemed to strike him most about his new station in life, however, was that all the men in the firm wore this particular kind of loafer, which comes "in all colors. They wear them in black, brown, navy." As it happened, I knew the shoes very well; my father had worn the same kind for years, but this news didn't seem to please the young man one bit.

Remembering the do-your-own-thing sixties, I felt sorry for the guy and suggested that he didn't have to work for his father if it made him unhappy; that he lived in a free country and maybe he could work somewhere else, where he could at least wear shoes that he liked. Again I'd said the wrong thing. "You don't understand," he said, in that patiently contemptuous tone which as an adolescent I had used to explain the facts of life to my parents. "This is a great business, and it's my father's. I have to work there. It would be," he paused for the right word, "unpatriotic not to work there." Unpatriotic? This was getting interesting.

But then (I swear) he ordered the loafers in black, brown, and navy, and pulled out his charge card; our conversation was suddenly closed. He didn't want to hear what I had to say, didn't want to think about choices; he had no intention of striking out on his own. His dismay at the shoes had been feigned. In spite of his protests, he wanted to belong to the world those loafers represented to him. The shoes were a kind of magic for him, like Dorothy's slippers that clicked her back to Kansas. Those loafers in three colors would protect him, in this case from having to make adult decisions or take adult action on his own. Not that there's necessarily anything wrong with going to work in one's father's business—but his pretense at dismay, even directed toward a stranger, said something, too. Adulthood is hard work, and even he knew you can't sneak into it so easily, letting someone else make all the arrangements. After all, this guy can't go on forever pretending to despise his shoes and the life they stand for.

A familiar scene: A man on a movie screen stands with a hand on a younger man's shoulder. The young man is wearing a soldier's uniform, or maybe a tux, if it happens to be his wedding day. Sometimes he's waiting for a train. In any event, he is embarking on a new phase of his life, and the older man is proud. "You're a man now, son," he says, and his son returns the look levelly, as if, for the first time, they're sharing a moment as equals. Or a variation: A young woman is going to college, is wearing her first formal dress, or shows up at her parents' house with an infant in her arms. "Now you're a woman." A man I used to work with—he was twenty-seven or twenty-eight—recently announced to his parents his plan to move back "home" for a while in order to save the money he was paying in rent so that he could buy some land. To his amazement, they said no. "It never occurred to me that they'd say no," he told me. "I mean, I'm their kid." But they'd given him the "now you're an adult" lecture, and that was that.

The myth here is that childhood and adulthood are on either side of a developmental Iron Curtain; once you cross the line, you can never go home again. Think of the phrase "separating the men from the boys," as if the transformation could be visible to the naked eye. Last week you were a boy, but now, completely and irrevocably, you're an adult. As my Wall Street acquaintance might have hoped, the idea is that grown-up shoes will make the man.

Perhaps I'm reading more into this man's psyche than I have a right to, but my guess is that through the shoes he was seeking something I've wished for for years: a symbolic rite of passage that would automatically transform me into an adult, change me inside and out, once and for all. If I were an adult, I figure, then I'd feel different, be able to live more easily with the choices I make, be more comfortable in my own life. Or if I were an adult maybe I could simply live, without the burden of my private questions slowing things down all the time. However, if adulthood were that automatic and simple, grown-up shoes *would* make the man. On the other hand, if it isn't that simple, what then is adulthood? How do you recognize an adult if not by his or her shoes, or accomplishments, or outlook? How does this "now you're a man" myth apply to my life or yours?

To define adulthood, I conducted an informal sur-

vey, which consisted of asking various people I knew—
some young, some not so young—what they thought
an adult was. It yielded answers that, under the surface
anyway, approached the issue from every angle. "An
adult is somebody who, when eating alone, doesn't do
it standing up and uses a plate"; "You're a grown-up
when you're accountable to yourself"; "If you don't
keep your socks under the bed." "Well," says another
friend with an admittedly convoluted approach, "I
never buy wine or Scotch because I only drink gin and
tonic. But when my friends come over, they never want
gin. I guess I'd be a grown-up if I bought what my
friends like, not just what I like." Someone else I talked
to thinks a grown-up is someone who can buy cookies
and not eat the whole package at once.

Others cited the responsibilities of children or car
payments, success, marriage, or a mortgage; or the
physical signs of aging, the awareness of mortality,
wanting to be alone, wanting not to be alone. There
were answers that had to do with wearing seatbelts
(grown-ups do), not listening to rock music all the time
(grown-ups don't), and how often an adult should wear
jeans (less often than kids). A good number of people
were in the "I hope I never find out" school. A twenty-
five-year-old woman I asked was almost hostile when
she asked in return, "Why are you asking *me*?" Not her
problem, she explained, she's just a kid. But a kid with
a live-in lover, a job, and a life full of other responsibilities.

Like the man with the shoes, all these people were
looking for—or were afraid of—the passage or commitment to adulthood. And also like the man with the
shoes, they all believed that adulthood would, like

puberty or death or a birthday, arrive unmistakably, when they had become whatever person they wanted to be. Adulthood was like the man or woman of one's dreams: No one knew what he or she would look like, but surely everyone would know when the right person came along.

My friend with the Scotch-drinking friends, for example, associates being a successful, expansive host with adulthood; as long as he keeps only his bottle of gin on hand, he can still think of himself, at thirty-four, as a kid, just having the other kids over: You can't fail as a host—or a grown-up—if you don't claim to be one. The woman who eats standing up (and who hasn't?) associates adulthood with decorum. Grown-ups, she believes, take care of themselves and eat proper meals. She's not quite ready for that yet. My guess is that if she learned to eat sitting down, there'd be another hurdle (real adults make their beds every day? real adults always pay their bills on time?) preventing her from becoming really, finally, adult.

I guess I was about twenty-one or twenty-two when all of a sudden it became clear to me that it was no longer appropriate to call either of my parents collect, except in emergencies. I don't remember whether my parents paused in disapproval before accepting the charges when I did call collect, or whether I decided to express my independence by calling directly, but I do know that I took this change in procedure seriously. I remember that there was a slight shift in relations all around at first, an awkwardness when I heard my voice say hello before I was introduced by the operator. (This change in procedure must have unsettled them, too.) And I can recall that I sometimes still longed to reverse the charges, though I wouldn't, because calling collect had always made me feel cared-for, protected. Even so, paying for the occasional phone call didn't make me the adult I'd hoped it would.

A few years later I had another false alarm. When I was twenty-seven, the wise folks at American Express decided that I was an adult. I'd applied for a card many times before, but this time, after countless of their "you've got to be kidding" rejection letters, they sent me a credit card, which seemed to me a real symbol of adulthood. Nothing about my precarious financial situation had changed, so I figured that they must know something about me that I didn't. I went out first thing and charged a leather credit-card case, which to this day I've never used, and my first night as a cardholder I took a friend out for an expensive dinner that I couldn't afford—the way it's done in the commercials—as though adulthood were somehow conferred along with credit. But I still didn't feel grown-up, really. For a long time I felt self-conscious about using the card, as if I were pretending to be a grown-up and likely to be caught in my act by an astute waiter or salesclerk.

I'd also imagined that the transformation into adulthood might coincide with a birthday—my twenty-first, twenty-fifth, then thirtieth—but I've given up on that. The first briefcase I ever owned was a grand symbol of adulthood, and for a while I firmly believed that a person with such a distinguished briefcase was surely an adult, but pretty soon a Bic pen leaked in it, leaving a stain that showed inside and out, and I went back to carrying my junk around in a canvas shoulder bag. At various times I've felt especially decisive or womanly or sexual, and there's something of adulthood in those qualities, but the metamorphosis has never come, not even now as I write this book.

I've thought adulthood might happen with marriage, but adulthood's private. To be able to make commitments is obviously an important component of adulthood, but, as many a married couple has discovered, commitments in themselves do not transform someone who's not an adult into someone who is. I've thought that adulthood might come with having a child, until I asked a friend with a two-year-old about it. "When Angela was first born," he said, "I was so proud; I did feel grown-up, maybe for the first time. I was thirty-five, and I remember I bought a filing cabinet. I was thinking that a person who's a father should be organized, have his 'affairs' in order. I thought, 'I have to take care of this little girl.' But then you think about wars and terrorism, and muggers—and you begin to feel insecure. There's no way to get your affairs that much in order. How can anyone be grown-up enough?" Without knowing it, he'd just put his finger on the catch-22 of adulthood.

In preindustrial Western culture there was no such thing as adulthood. Strange as this may seem, there were no adults (nor were there such things as middle age or adolescence—but more on that later); as an "official" stage of life, adulthood was simply never an issue as such. You were a man or a woman if you weren't a child, that's all, and the difference for men was one of size, age, and physical capacity; girls became women when they became fertile. Being adult had little to do with wisdom, opportunity, accountability, or a superior knowledge of the world, as it does now. The invention of adulthood is a recent one—and because its definition is still evolving (and will continue to do so) it's hard to know, as my friend put it, when you've grown up "enough." Adulthood as we know it has its minimum requirements, but no end of possibilities.

Imagine, for example, that you were a tailor, or a tailor's wife, in early seventeenth-century England.* For all practical purposes, your craft or your husband's would set you up for life. Your father had very likely been a tailor, your name may even have been Taylor, your social class was that of a tailor, your household was organized like a tailor's, and as your children watched you sew, they knew they'd grow up to be tailors, too, unless a daughter married a Smith or a Baker, which amounted to the same thing. Had you been of the upper class, or a lower class, your life would have been circumscribed in the same way, though either more or less comfortably. "In my little town I never meant nothing / I was just my father's son," Paul Simon grieves in one of his songs. But it wasn't so long ago that that was the whole point.

There were slight variations on the theme. If the tailor had five sons, not all of them could inherit the shop. Some would be shipped off as early as the age of seven to be apprenticed to another tailor, or a smith or baker. (So much for sentimental ideas of the loving, tight-knit families of old.) Our original Taylor would bring in apprentices (something like our exchange students) to work for him, to compensate for his faraway

* Maybe you think you have nothing in common with a tailor from seventeenth-century England, but you do.

sons-in-training. Occasionally a clergyman would take a special interest in a tradesman's particularly gifted son and arrange for his education. Almost anything could happen (at least if you were a boy), but mostly very little happened: The tailor's son grew up to be a tailor, his daughter a tailor's wife, and that was that.

The conflicts of young Taylor's life would have been very different from ours. Certainly there were philosophical issues to speculate about—God and the Devil, life and death—and surely some tailors must have dreamed of other lives, yet in such traditional societies ordered to the neat parade of generations and tailors' shops, the gap between childhood and adulthood was practically nonexistent. The passage through life was not traumatic: You'd been trained all your life to take over.

Children are always taught the superstitions, fears, and possibilities of their worlds—and the imagination can stretch only so far. Young Taylor might have longed to travel, explore, or learn to read, but it would not have occurred to him that he could create for himself the life he wanted, down to the last detail, the way we are expected to today: What should I do for a living? Where should I live? Should I marry or not? Should I come out of the closet? Do I want children? Should I take a share in a ski house this winter? Should I become a blonde? Do I need an MBA? What would make me happy? The guy in the shoestore worried about working for his father instead of making his own way in the world; young Taylor might instead have worried about abandoning his father's tailor shop.

Take away choice, and sooner or later you'll take away the desire to choose. The orderliness of Taylor's world kept him in check. He would have worried about such real things as disease, war, famine, fire—his world was by no means idyllic or safe—and, because war, famine, fire, and disease were beyond his control, he would have looked for comfort elsewhere, in magic, religion, or witchcraft, something he hoped could control what he himself couldn't, not unlike children today, who grow up believing that grown-ups know and can take care of everything. Young Taylor wouldn't have ascribed special powers to the grown-ups around him. What could they do to protect him from disease, war, fire, or famine? They might be bigger than he was but still not big enough. Nobody was big enough.

By the end of the seventeenth century, however, being adult began little by little to mean something more than being a grown child. The Oxford English Dictionary cites the first use of the word *manhood* in the thirteenth century and of *womanhood* a century after that. Manhood meant strength, virtue, the courage to fight for one's own, and all that; womanhood encompassed the dark mysteries of childbearing, gentleness, the nurturing instincts, and so on. Six centuries ago, one knew what men and women were. But an adult?

In adulthood lies something else, something harder to pinpoint: a measure of control, the capacity to use your freedoms and reserves of inner strength, a way of participating in and knowing the world. Autonomy, the freedom and responsibility to make your own choices, live your own life—autonomy that transcends gender. Manhood and womanhood in the conventional sense happen more or less automatically, and we all become grown-ups when we're old enough, but adulthood is something to reach for—maybe it's the only thing that makes being a grown-up make sense. The idea of "becoming" adult in this way first shows up, though vaguely, in the OED in 1656, when the adult was described as having ". . . come to his full ripeness, force and bigness." The word *adulthood,* used almost reverently as we would use it today, does not make its first distinct appearance in the dictionary until 1870—which in historical terms is like the day before yesterday.

What this means is that adulthood came to denote what men and women achieved once the world of fixed values, which Western man had known more or less until the seventeenth century, gave way to a world of greater possibilities. As people began to travel, learn, and emerge from the straitjacket medieval world of the Taylors, Western humankind suddenly grew bigger, physically and spiritually. Little by little, man, and increasingly man's machines, took on many of God's powers (to say nothing of the Devil's). Bit by bit, as our ancestors began to control the previously uncontrollable, they themselves assumed a new importance in their own world. Grown-ups now knew more than they ever had before; children, by comparison, knew much less, and the gap between childhood and adulthood widened. No longer did God (or the Devil or local witch) decide whether a child's infection would fester or be cured; now a doctor, a human being, could have a say in the matter. As God and the unknowable receded, his subjects asserted themselves; the world looked different. Over the centuries, the adult—more and more responsible for his own destiny—came to be "invented."

That the first glimpse of adulthood appears in our

language in 1656 is significant, for the history of adulthood really begins with the history of America, and by this time our Puritan ancestors were in their New World heyday, in fact beginning their decline.

The god of these Puritans was a new kind of god, one who, unlike the paternalistic god of the Church of England, gave mankind a little more choice. The Puritans' god, like the gods of the many other versions of Christianity that emerged during the Reformation, did not entirely control man's destiny. What these new religions had in common—and you can understand why this shook things up—was that for the first time man was to share the responsibility for his life with God. What's more, as time went on, he would become increasingly free to choose whichever god pleased him.

This slow secularizing process, the shifting of power from god to man, enabled—indeed forced—man to take over the wheel of his own life. Now young Taylor could do anything he wanted; he could trade in his stern, unyielding god for a more permissive one and, at the same time, trade in his social order for one more to his liking, especially if the god he chose advised him to head for the New World. Now he didn't have to be a Taylor if he chose not to be. He could farm his own land, become a preacher, or one day President. (As for poor Mrs. Taylor, she still had the raw end of the deal, as usual.)

The Puritan settlers who headed for these shores to escape religious persecution had nothing against acquiring land, making money, setting up a new life away from the rigid social system of England—and in turn persecuting later groups who also came to the New World in search of "religious" freedom. Generous they were not. Our Pilgrims had an "I got here first—it's mine" attitude, and never mind the Indians. The Puritans were very much in the American grain, as it turned out. Strengthened by their faith that their righteous god knew right from wrong, and further strengthened by the fact that this was a new god who made up rules as (s)he went along, they were now free to do pretty much what they wanted. The problem was, they were uncomfortable with this new freedom. Given the strict world from which they had come, they were terrified to find themselves responsible for their own lives. Soon, they had made too many rules for themselves and forced others to break away from them as they had broken away from the Church of England. And so they eventually lost control of the world they had found—but not without leaving a legacy. Under the groups that followed them, the power in America would shift even more from god to man.

To put it simply, the Old World was no longer big enough to contain the energies of an expanding population in search of possibilities, of a people becoming more hopeful and ambitious about what life might bring. Thus there arose new ideas about God, new ideas about man's destiny, new ideas about the state and human freedom—ideas that showed what God-fearing, disciplined, hard-working men could expect from life—and what he (and later she) could expect, out there on his own, was not an orderly progression to a preordained role in the world but the right and duty to find his own way: in other words, adulthood.

Perhaps I'm being hard on the Puritans: I don't mean to suggest that they trekked all the way across the ocean just to be free to take land that didn't belong

to them and make money, for they did take their religion seriously. However, they were also grappling
with unfamiliar freedom, with the seeds of that autonomy we now think of as adulthood. First a little knowledge of the physical world opens your eyes to all there
is yet to be learned, then religious freedom, then the
freedom to live and work where you want; then comes
the freedom to disengage yourself from your past,
from the status conferred by your birth, and finally
you are free, in principle anyway, to challenge fate itself, a right that two centuries later seemed to William
James as natural as breathing. Next thing you know
(and this might have given the Puritans a chuckle),
you're blinded by the challenge of a world that's supposed to be yours for the taking, and wondering what
in God's (or whomever's) name you're supposed to do
with your life, now that the decision is yours. Each of
us, as we come of age, is like a settler landing for the
first time on the Plymouth Rock of his or her life, starting fresh. There are times when I suppose all of us
would rather be Taylors.

Where Taylor looked to his parents, his social system, his community, and his god to find out how to set
up his life, the Puritans broke away from their history,
created new communities and new social structures,
and relied on their god and themselves for the rest. As
for us, our families are scattered, our communities are
not of the you-build-my-barn, I'll-build-yours kind, our
social system is wide open, and, unless we decide to become fundamentalist Christians or Moonies, any gods
we may worship are not likely to make the rules by
which we'll be able to get through the day.

In a pinch, Taylor would have asked himself, "What

does God want me to do?" The Puritans would have asked, "What should I do, and how will God judge me?" But in a world where neither God nor our social structure nor our parents are likely to supply the answer, we ask instead: "What should I do?" For better and worse, we look for the answers in what we call adulthood.

| 3 |

FALSE STANDARDS

I remember my mother's thirtieth birthday very well. My father had worked for a string of large corporations—GE, Ford, etc.—and with every promotion we moved to a new city, on an average of once a year. We were living in Philadelphia when my mother turned thirty. It was January, and it was cold, as cold as it had been the winter before, when we'd lived in Portland, Maine. My father was away on a business trip.

We lived in a suburb called Plymouth Meeting, on a curved street in a split-level house, a house that looked like every other house on the block, though it was bigger than the house we'd moved from (and not as big as the house we'd move to next, in suburban Connecticut). My mother knew no one; she hadn't been, and wouldn't be, in Philadelphia long enough to make many friends, although the sadness of this didn't occur to me then. She spent her birthday, the big "three-oh," cooped up in this unfamiliar house with her three small daughters; we all had colds. She wept and tried to explain to us why she was weeping, but we were all under ten and none of us understood. Otherwise, we might have thought she was right to cry. To little kids, turning thirty sounds very close to death.

I also remember my own thirtieth birthday. Like most of my friends, and many of my statistical contemporaries, I was unmarried, had no children, and lived not in a "starter" house as my parents had done, but in a one-person apartment in New York. I had spent the ten years or so that my parents had spent as "young marrieds," respectively, in school, living with roommates, then with a man, then alone—and in several jobs before I found one I liked. I'd been trying out adulthood but without committing to it—nor had adulthood made me any irresistible offers. And at thirty, this memory of my mother's birthday came back to me. Mother and daughter, but for all we had in common we might as well have come from different centuries or different planets.

On my birthday, I cried too. The difference was that, at thirty, my mother felt burdened by too many responsibilities—husband, children, cleaning, meals to cook on time, missing buttons and unmatched socks—while I was only beginning to feel the very different burden of a life without such responsibilities. My only burden was me—but at thirty such a life, for all its exhilaration, can be painful too. For one thing, it can seem pointless. On this benchmark birthday, my mother mistakenly thought her life was over. In a different world, I wondered when my adult life would begin.

*   *   *

When I was writing this book and someone asked what it was about, I would answer, and ask in return, "What were your parents doing when they were your age?" Among my postwar friends, the answer was almost always along the same lines: "Um, well, you know. They were ahead of me in some ways—they were married and had their kids; they owned a house by now. They were different: They were real grown-ups." Or, "They were divorced by now and I'm not even married yet"; "My daughter is two—when my mother was my age I was seventeen!"; "My father was a vice president by now, and at the office I'm still considered one of the kids"; or even, "I'm doing better in some ways—I mean, I have a job I like and I don't think my father liked his." Rarely, however, were my friends following their parents' lead.

I'd never realized before how naturally—even unconsciously—we all measure our lives against our parents'. I know, I know: You never wanted to grow up to be like your parents; no one does. Even so, the agenda by which they lived is the agenda you grew up taking for granted, believing it was what adulthood was all about. If your career is longer in taking off than your father's was (or more rarely, your mother's), perhaps you feel a little behind schedule; if you still live in an apartment that feels like a college dorm, while at your age your parents had a four-bedroom house on an acre of land, you might wonder if you'll ever catch up. Or you want your two kids to have their own rooms and now they share one. It's unsettling if your parents married at twenty-three but here you are, thirty-three, and you don't even have any friends who are married yet.

And so on. Or maybe your parents just seemed more at home in grown-up bodies and lives than you think you ever will. Most of us assume that our parents had adulthood down pat, and either we measure up or we don't.

If you believe much of the media coverage about us, we don't measure up. (And how the media love to measure us! As *Time* magazine said recently, the postwar generation has been "relentlessly scrutinized, dissected and classified" from infancy on, not least by *Time* itself.) According to various accounts, we're the "postponed" generation, "downwardly mobile," suffering from the "Peter Pan syndrome," in general spoiled, narcissistic yuppies who refuse to face up to the real responsibilities of adulthood. Nonsense. If the media would instead scrutinize, dissect, and classify not our generation but the patterns of adulthood that have been emerging in this country over the last hundred years, they would see something else. Our mistake is in comparing ourselves to our parents' generation: *It was the baby-boom parents—and not their children—who profoundly distorted the patterns of modern adulthood that have been shaping America since the mid-nineteenth century.* My thirtieth birthday was perfectly in keeping with the long-term American pattern. It was my mother's birthday, as we'll see, that was out of step.

When I think of the way my life is now, or how varied the lives of my friends are, I see all over again the sameness of the cookie-cutter lives from which most of my friends and I emerged: suburban house with bikes in the driveway, TV in the family room, barbecue grill on the patio, hunts in the morning for misplaced commuter tickets, cupboards full of breakfast cereals in many flavors, a station wagon. Not that families didn't have their squabbles and private miseries and worse, but they occurred in the setting of a home and family. As has often been pointed out, the America I grew up in had reached a state of "normalcy" that was so rigid it was downright weird. This was normalcy with a vengeance. And it couldn't last.

I try now to imagine my mother at twenty-one, pregnant with me, married to my father, who turned twenty-four a few weeks before I was born. I wonder what it was like for them as children growing up in the Depression, though neither of them suffered nearly as much as so many of their contemporaries. Still, they cannot have been unmarked by those grim times because, like the rest of their generation, they came of age with an unusually deep need for security. Back in the fifties, the economist John Kenneth Galbraith called the widespread fear of another depression "Depression Psychosis," and another historian wrote of the mid-fifties: "No matter the rampant boom, no matter that during all the years since the beginning of World War II most families had been prospering; the edginess about a possible depression continued." My parents' generation had been badly scarred by 25-percent unemployment, by breadlines, by business failures, and then by the horrors of World War II. By 1945, when the War was over and they had come of age, they were more than ready to settle down.

I try to picture my parents as teenagers during the Second World War, my father joining the navy at seventeen, claiming to be eighteen, and my mother rolling Red Cross bandages on Cape Cod, where she grew up and where residents had to use blackout curtains at night, lest a German submarine come ashore. I try to imagine them cheering when the bombs went off over Hiroshima and Nagasaki, thrilled, like the rest of America, that the War was over, that we and nobody else had these wonderful bombs, and that, with the Depression and War behind us, everything might finally be okay at last—or in the words of a famous wartime song, "There'll be love and laughter / And peace ever after / Tomorrow, when the world is free."

I've always been puzzled when I hear references to the optimism that my parents' young generation took with them to their new suburban homes after the War and that encouraged them to start families when they themselves were barely out of childhood. How, with all that had so recently happened—the War, the Holocaust, the bomb—could they have been so *optimistic*? Hopeful, I could understand, or warily trusting, or maybe it took a long time for the reality of the death camps and the bomb to sink in—but optimistic? When I try to imagine the early years of the baby boom—the Korean War, the Red-baiting, again the shadow of the bomb—I picture a party where everything has gone wrong and where, even so, through clenched teeth, guests and hosts alike pretend that the party is going fine. When I think of my parents' generation, I can't help feeling that the optimism that fostered the baby boom was partly, or maybe largely, a matter of relief on the part of the survivors and despair at what their survival had cost, and not a spontaneous or genuine revival of spirits. Nevertheless, my parents and the other members of their generation vaulted into adulthood and accepted its discipline with an agility and indifference to the consequences that only the very young possess.

*   *   *

I can remember very clearly meeting a college friend of my father's when I must have been about eight or nine. He was single, and though I was hardly the most sheltered kid who ever lived, I was horrified by his plight—no wife, no normal home, no children. I don't think I had ever met anyone so exotic as an unmarried grown-up before. During his visit, my sisters and I, not fighting for once, furiously colored pictures from our coloring books for him, so that he could stick them on his refrigerator with magnets and *pretend* he had kids; we assumed this would make him feel better. Later, I thought about him a lot: Why was this nice man not married? It never occurred to me that living alone could have been what he preferred or that he may, for, uh, other reasons, have chosen to forgo women and children.

That I was so saddened by his solitude makes me laugh now, but even at that early age I had internalized the bizarre norms of the time: In the generation of baby-boom parents, a record-breaking 96 percent of all men and women of marriageable age, including homosexuals, as they were then called (if they were referred to at all), and loners and many other people who never should have tried family life, got married—and on the average they married earlier than any other generation in our history. A few years after the War, more Americans than ever before owned their own houses. A higher percentage of couples than ever before had kids, and kids in greater quantities than families had had since the century before. Like my parents, many bore their families at an unusually early age. Even older women, who in large numbers had waited out the War to have their children at the last minute, were having babies; during the baby boom there were actually two generations of families changing diapers at the same time. And unprecedented numbers of women gave up the educational and professional gains that earlier generations of women had achieved over the past fifty years to stay in their homes and raise their families. No wonder that, like my postwar contemporaries, I grew up believing that the normal adult married and often married early, had children automatically, and so on. Adulthood had never been like this before, however—not for my grandparents, or theirs—and will never be this way again.

Compare, for example, the 96 percent of people in my parents' generation who got married with the one-third of eligible American men and women in 1900 who never married. In the 1850s, marriages most often took place between ages twenty-five and thirty; in 1890, the average man married at twenty-six, the average woman at twenty-four. Between 1900 and 1950, only about half the women in this country aged twenty to twenty-four were married, but *three-quarters* of women of that age had married by 1960. In 1956 the median age for women to marry was twenty, and for men twenty-two, the lowest in America's history. By 1960, half the women getting married in this country were still in their teens: The normal woman was a child bride.

Now take the baby-boom generation. Among women aged twenty to twenty-four, *half are married*: In that respect we've returned precisely to what was considered normal before our parents inflated the numbers. The median ages for marriage today are twenty-five for men and twenty-three for women, though many more of us—and don't forget, there are many more of us to begin with—are marrying much later. Actually, we marry most often at about the same age as the colonists in Massachusetts 300 years ago: On the whole, we're not postponing marriage; it was our parents who jumped the gun.

Seventy-five percent of us will marry. That sounds low, compared to our parents' staggering 96 percent, but let's put the figure in context. Some estimates, for example, argue that as many as 10 percent of us to-day—and in higher numbers among baby boomers—are living out-of-the-marriage-market gay lives, there-by removing themselves from the accounting. Add to that the number of people living together but not mar-ried, four times as many now as before 1970, and you can eliminate still more of us from the contest. What's more, women with college educations traditionally marry less than do their peers who did not attend col-lege. (In 1952, for example, college graduates married at one-third the rate of those who had not attended college.) Since today a higher percentage of women than ever before are college graduates and profes-sionals, our "low" marital rates must be adjusted even further. Finally, at least a percentage point or two of us prefer not to marry, and, living as we do in a time when that choice is socially acceptable, that preference should also be figured into the accounting. Thus the rate at which we'll marry is *not* unnaturally low—there is no widespread "marriage bust"—and, again, we are perfectly in keeping with prewar trends.

As to the numbers of women in my parents' genera-tion having children and the number of children they were having, the birthrate, with slight fluctuations, had begun to drop about 1850 and stayed on the low side until 1946. The baby-boom mothers in fact had more children than any generation had had since 1885 (when the infant mortality rate was higher and many families still favored lots of children to work their farms). Twenty-two percent of women born in 1908 never had children at all, while only 8 percent of those born in the 1930s—again, the baby-boom mothers— were childless. The percentage of families with two or more children rose during the baby-boom years from 55 to 82 percent. Furthermore, blacks (who traditionally had more children, but whose fertility rates had also been going down since the nineteenth century), Jews, educated women and urban women (who traditionally had fewer children), and Catholics and rural women (who traditionally had more children) all conformed to the giddy baby-boom pattern: The number of children, and the ages at which women had them, were fairly consistent from religion to religion and from social class to social class.

The easy explanation for this family euphoria was that these new postwar families were uncommonly optimistic and eager to get on with "normal" life once the Depression and the War were over. Yet postwar prosperity and optimism are not in themselves sufficient explanations for the baby boom; throughout the wildly prosperous and euphoric twenties, for example, which also followed a world war, the birthrate went down sharply; 22 percent of women born around 1900, remember, never had children at all, and the birthrate in the twenties was much lower than it is today, even with all the talk about our recent "baby bust."

In addition to this famous postwar optimism, two

considerably more down-to-earth factors can help to explain the national baby craze. The first was the G.I. Bill, with its long list of benefits for veterans—free tuition, cheap mortgages, insurance, loans to start businesses, allowances for G.I. wives and kids—all of which encouraged marriage and family life. The second was the Highway Act of 1944, which publicly funded roads around and between cities—the very roads that made the new suburbs, with their uniform, cheap government-financed housing possible. What started the baby boom rolling, then, was money from the government, money which kept rolling in long after the War was over. It was this same money that made men marry and women willingly drop out of the work force. It sponsored the new wave of home ownership, and it subsidized, among other things, my two sisters and me.

That the government got the money by borrowing it for future generations—including mine—to repay also helps explain why my parents could afford a house more cheaply than I can afford an apartment: Today, the national debt exceeds $2 trillion, and a share of the interest on that $2 trillion is added to my tax bill (and yours) each year. Between 1940 and 1960, home ownership rose more than 100 percent, thanks partly to government money that made it possible for the first time in our history for more people to own than to rent their homes. Home ownership has always been an American dream, but that's all it was, a dream, something to strive for—the way it is now—but when our parents came of age, houses, cars, spouses, and babies were practically presents from the government, which helps explain that generation's optimism. For a few years, anyway.

*   *   *

One thing led to another. The birthrate stayed high
(over 4 million babies a year) until 1964, when, according to most experts, the baby boom "officially" came to
an end, which also happens to be the time we escalated
the Vietnam War. Coincidence? I don't think so. Birth-
rates may rise during brief wars, but they decline during protracted wars, even though, early on, we were
reluctant to consider Vietnam a "real" war. By 1964,
optimism was no longer in the wind—another reason
for the birthrate to fall: Moral issues aside, this was a
real war, and even then it was clear—on some level—
that it was not going to have a happy ending. Soon
there would be talk of another depression, or worse.
And suddenly there were other reasons for us to question ourselves and our future.

In 1965, "Death and the Mid-life Crisis" by Eliott
Jacques was published in the *International Journal of Psychoanalysis*. The article, which would prove to be extremely influential, first introduced the term "mid-life
crisis," and used as case studies the lives of more than
300 artists, composers, writers, poets, and sculptors—
Shakespeare, Goethe, Beethoven, and Gauguin, for example—who had come to intense realizations about life
and death somewhere between thirty-five and thirty-
nine, and as a result had transformed their lives and
their art, for better or worse.

My mother would have been thirty-six in 1965, and
my father thirty-eight. (And I wouldn't be surprised if
Jacques had been about the same age himself.) Until
now, conformity had been the theme of their generation; you did what everyone else did, stayed in line, but
no sooner had Jacques published his article than this

mid-life affliction that he described became a self-fulfilling prophecy. To one extent or another, soon everyone in my parents' generation would be having a mid-life crisis. By 1968, for example, my father had given up a successful corporate career to start his own business and a new life in the Caribbean, leaving my mother, my sisters, and me behind, as if he were Gauguin himself. Later my "stay-at-home" mother would also turn her life around, remarry, open a shop, and become mayor of the town in which she eventually settled down. The message that reached my parents and (if not as sensationally) everyone else in America by the mid-sixties was that the dutiful lives they had been living up until then were not their only choice. Thus a new, if disruptive, dimension was added to a generational life cycle that, as we've seen, had already shown considerable deviance.

When my parents came of age, "maturity" was the catchword, just as "fulfillment" would be a catchword of the sixties and seventies. The baby-boom parents had had no adolescence to speak of, not as their children would define it—no time to hang out, to experiment with possible lives. What they had wanted was just to get safely into port as soon as possible. Writer Maureen Howard remembers: "We had no position, no place in the world and never stopped to take much pleasure in our youth. Our beauty and freedom were ignored while we yearned for the goods of dissatisfied middle age." Premature, dissatisfied middle age. By 1965, however, thanks to the reawakening Jacques had encouraged, our parents now wanted a little of the pleasure and freedom they had postponed for so long.

As if to dramatize the changes in the air, the oldest

baby-boom kids began going to college in record numbers in 1965, give or take a couple of years, and, to the music of the Beatles and the Rolling Stones, and with the writings of Kerouac and Salinger to guide them, the youth movement picked up steam. These kids, rich and free compared to what their parents had been, were coming of age in a world that, for all its material comforts, had suddenly turned threatening—Dallas, Vietnam, peace marches, race riots. Where their parents had tried to find order in the appearance of maturity and conformity, these kids could see that those efforts had instead produced a kind of chaos. They saw they'd have to live their lives differently.

The contempt that their children were now so openly directing at them couldn't help but reinforce Jacques's message to baby-boom parents. Like my father, they might look at the junk they'd piled up over the years—for what? The fathers, the men, might have forgotten by now the thrill of their first good job; now doctors began telling them not to work so hard, to slow down, watch the blood pressure. The mothers, the women, must have been saddened by the suddenly hostile kids for whom they had given up their youth, their careers, and their egos. Beginning in 1960, one million women a year, for economic and other reasons, began leaving their homes to go to work. And it was, after all, Betty Friedan and her contemporaries who created today's feminist movement, not some upstart baby-boom college girl who hadn't yet discovered the hazards of a sexist world.

By the mid-sixties, even the TV sitcoms had begun to reflect the changed world; "normal" family life went off the air. *Ozzie and Harriet* and *The Donna Reed Show,* both long-running programs, disappeared in 1966, the same year *That Girl,* with a feisty Marlo Thomas trying to make her way as a single woman in the world, was introduced. By 1970 the "normal" American TV family was the Odd Couple or Mary Tyler Moore, living alone. It was too late for my parents' generation to mold itself back into history, but it was clear by now that adulthood as they had interpreted it early on was a shambles.

Other factors coalesced about this time. The sequence itself is not important here. The point instead is that the youth movement had its counterpart in a grown-up revolt, and it's my argument that the two revolts played off each other and that neither would have happened without the other. Which came first is a chicken-and-egg question. It's significant, for example, that mass therapy—along with drugs, all the consciousness-raising panaceas, and the human potential movement—became big business at this time. Fulfillment, which had hardly been mentioned by my parents' generation as a criterion for maturity, now became, for the first time in America's history (or anyone's), a middle-class obsession.

Where once our parents' generation had blindly pursued premature "dissatisfied middle age," now they were buying contact lenses, leisure suits, go-go boots, and sporty new Mustang convertibles. "I remember very clearly," says a friend, "how we all laughed at my father—I don't know, sometime in the sixties—when he bought a pair of plaid pants, for playing golf. Madras pants, they seemed so funny." Not so funny— and not long after the plaid pants her father began having an affair, she later learned. Work, marriage, sex, life suddenly all had to be fulfilling. Barbara Ehrenreich, in *The Hearts of Men*, analyzes the fifties and sixties: "Where the life cycle had been seen as a quick climb leading to the plateau of maturity, there was now an endlessly upward-curving arc," no end to the possibilities for fulfillment. Divorce was now a "growth experience" instead of a disaster or a shameful family secret; getting fired could be life-enhancing. Masturbation, according to another observer, which had once been a disease, now was a cure. And as Ehrenreich points out, to be unhappy came to mean being unhealthy. You owed it to yourself to do something about it.

In addition, demographers at the time had begun to notice something peculiar. While America was youth-heavy at one end of the scale, we were gaining fast at the other end. Statistically, many more of us were living much, much longer. Those of us born directly after the War, for example, have a life expectancy six years longer than those born just before the War—a mere four years earlier—and the life-expectancy gains had been dramatic since the turn of the century. Here was another message for postwar parents: Life wasn't so short after all. Maybe they had grown up—or acted the part—too early. So why not make up for it now? The idea was surely subliminal, but just as their kids were growing older (if fighting it), many of their postwar parents were going in the other direction: growing younger—experimenting sexually or sartorially, reading Betty Friedan or getting a hair transplant, or simply reordering their responsible lives to include, for once, themselves.

So where did that leave their kids, the darlings of a

shattered dream? For one thing, it left us with badly mixed signals about what grown-up life was supposed to be like. Not only had we internalized a version of normal adulthood that was statistically as well as practically abnormal, but now our parents, the exemplars of this norm, had in large numbers and in all sorts of ways given up this impossible norm themselves. Mothers who had lovingly taught their little girls to bake cookies, for example, were now telling them, often with a trace of bitterness, not to jump into marriage so selflessly, to think about a career. And fathers were hinting to their sons, also with a trace of bitterness, that a safe job wasn't everything, after all.

It left us, together with—and at odds with—our "reborn" parents, facing a changed world none of us saw was coming. The postwar party was over.

| 4 |

SOME CHILDHOODS

Early in the spring of 1968, when I was a junior in high school, a friend of mine called Rachael invited me to her house one afternoon—to study, she said. I didn't want to go, because Rachael had seemed remote lately, not only to me but to the rest of us who hung around together at that time. She no longer wanted to paint signs for our varsity pep rallies; she had stopped ironing her hair, so it frizzed out now, and she had renounced the pastel skirts and sweaters the rest of us wore and had taken to wearing loose black clothing. Months before, she had begun to avoid our slumber parties, and even our parties with boys, because plainly they bored her. She was going out with someone in college, we knew, and we attributed the changes in her to his influence, or to the ups and downs of love. She was unusually friendly that day, though, so I went home with her.

Rachael's mother was out; we had the house to ourselves. Gathering up some junk food, we settled into Rachael's bedroom, turned on the stereo, opened the windows, and lit forbidden cigarettes. I'd always loved her room: the pink-frilled canopied bed, flowered wallpaper with matching fabric on the dressing-table skirt, a pink bulletin board cluttered with postcards, ribbons she'd won, and various ticket stubs, photographs, and cartoons. The room reflected the teenager with whom I felt at home and not this disapproving stranger in black who sat curled up Indian-style on her bed, eating potato chips with one hand and with her other hand absently stroking a stuffed white bunny called Jamie who lived perched on her pink pillows. The new Rachael got right down to business. We weren't there to study, as it turned out, not in the conventional sense.

What she was to tell me was secret, she said, our other friends were not to know: Her boyfriend was a member of SDS. From the hushed tone of her voice I knew this was major news, so I acted surprised—but SDS? (Something to do with Sammy Davis? The Settling Down Society? Start Driving Sooner?) I hadn't a clue what SDS was and was ashamed to ask. Rachael went on about all kinds of important things—I forget now what she said they were—that were going on in the world and how upset she was that none of her old friends were paying attention to them . . . and then she asked whether I'd like to skip school a few days later to go downtown with her to hear Robert Kennedy, who was running for President, give a speech. More confused than politically aroused, I said I would go.

I lived in a picture-perfect suburb of Detroit then—

hilly, winding streets with big houses set way back, pretty little lakes everywhere, for boating in summer and skating in winter—and had done so for almost two years, but I had never actually been to Detroit itself, only twenty or thirty miles away. "Downtown" was out of bounds. But Rachael, who picked me up in her car on the morning of our truancy, knew her way around admirably, and before long we were in an expansive park on the shore of Lake Michigan; I'd had no idea that downtown would be so close, so unthreatening, or, at least at the water's edge, so beautiful.

Over the exhilarated shouts and demands of the crowd—many young people, I noticed, and had they all skipped school, too?—we heard Kennedy speak. I don't remember what he said, but I do remember the excitement; I felt it, too. I could also feel the rage I had been hearing about lately—over Vietnam, civil rights, and over all the many things that were wrong—a rage that, up until then, hadn't seemed to have very much to do with me. Though this assembled crowd never got violent, it might have, and downtown, I now knew, wasn't so far from home.

I also learned what SDS was that day. Many of the people there were carrying signs, among them signs that spelled out Students for a Democratic Society. (That just puzzled me more: What else, I wondered, would students be for?) Except for their messages, the signs reminded me of the ones that decorated our high school gym during football and basketball pregame rallies, or maybe I just wanted them to be as safe as the spray-painted signs I already knew about.

We drove home later, back to Rachael's house to forge notes from our parents about why we hadn't been in school that day. A couple of months after that Robert Kennedy was assassinated. And from then on, whenever I tried to convince myself that the orderly world I had grown up knowing still made sense, I would remember Rachael, a young girl in her pink bedroom, eating potato chips, petting her stuffed animal, and trying to tell me otherwise.

Just as our parents—Rachael's, mine, and millions of others—had spent those early postwar years clinging to implausible standards of normalcy, so had Rachael and I, and millions of others, grown up believing in the same false standards: matching moms and dads, several kiddies' commuting distance away from the dads' offices, a strong, united country on the move, with a stable and worry-free future ahead. However we middle-class postwar kids imagined we'd improve upon this idyllic script as soon as we grew up ("I would never yell at my kids just for not making their beds!"), our fantasies were grounded in these false standards, this myth—which we kids didn't recognize as a myth; we mistook it for reality. If, as is often said, childhood is the rehearsal for adulthood, then we were rehearsing all along for the wrong show.

Not too long ago, I was asked to review a book about men and women who came of age in the fifties, called *Private Lives,* for the book page of a daily newspaper. I was eager to take on the assignment—it had about it the aura of "spying" on my parents and eavesdropping on my own early years—but I was also apprehensive: Who was I, after all, to review my parents' generation? I liked the book, and said so, but it also troubled me for some reason, and it was weeks after I'd turned in

my review before I realized why. The author, Benita
Eisler, had interviewed numerous adults of my parents'
age and had written an entire book about their lives in
the fifties and sixties with scarcely a mention, except in
passing, of their children! Apart from the occasional
reference to unsavory piles of diapers and the perennial shortage of babysitters in those years, the postwar
generation, the largest generation in our history, simply does not exist in *Private Lives*. "Starting out married, for most couples," Eisler writes, "was inseparable
from beginning life as parents." No big deal. My contemporaries and I, the famous baby boomers, were
nothing but casual background figures, props that
helped fill out the postwar dream.

To read *Private Lives* (to say nothing of much of the
other sociological literature about those years) is to see
that postwar America was not child-centered, as it was
often depicted: Instead, postwar America centered
around the larger myth—the myth of family; of
women and men behaving in certain ways; of suburban
houses, cars, washing machines, and, to use the catchword of the day, family "togetherness"; and the myth
of a packaged normalcy that was, in the words of an ad
I remember from my childhood, "whiter than white."
As for the children, whatever we might have been as
individuals, we were essential to the myth: If not for
us, why would houses need to be built, or fathers have
to work so hard, or so many mothers have to stay at
home to care for us? Without us, without the props,
the myth would have fallen apart much sooner.

I've always been reluctant to believe that we are who
we are because we were born when we were born; I
prefer to think that my problems are my own and not

shared by millions of others just like me. However, to
recall the way it was when I was growing up is to
understand the absolute and unnatural sameness of
middle-class life in those years, a sameness that, while it
lasted, filtered all the way down from our parents to
the youngest of us and that has, I believe, left its mark.
I can very clearly remember on any number of occasions going to the train station with my mother and
sisters to pick up my father after work; as the commuters disembarked, I'd go into a mild panic: All the
commuters looked the same, and how would we find
the right father? Who's to say it didn't work the other
way around as well? How were the fathers to find the
right wives and children? There were so many of us
kids—in those days Hitchcock could as easily have
made a horror film called *The Babies* as *The Birds*—and
despite the differences among us, we were all formed
by our parents, by the public schools, by the TV shows
we watched, by the same insubstantial myth.

There are good and bad and unique memories from
every childhood (obviously the common assumptions
of a generation are only some of them), but the collec-
tive experience of the postwar children foreshadowed
in unusually revealing ways the experiences we're sharing as adults, if for no other reason than that so many
of us grew up under the protective rules of the same
overpowering ethos. As a result, and thanks to the improved communications systems that made it easier to
transmit the fine points of the myth to every corner of
the country, we share more common experiences than
any generation has in the past. We were brought together by television, advertising, franchised stores and
services, unprecedented mobility, air travel, Dr. Spock,

Mr. Spock, Dick, Jane, Sally, and Spot; the oldest among us knew Captain Kangaroo and Mr. Greenjeans, and the youngest learned to read by watching *Sesame Street*. If a new fad started in Oregon, it wouldn't be long before it hit Kentucky. To feel at home in a new city, you'd just go to the nearest McDonald's. As a friend of mine who comes from the South says, with hardly a drawl, "My family has lived in Virginia for years and years, so I keep looking for my southern roots, thinking I'll find something out. But I really had a shopping-mall childhood just like everyone else I know."

What my friend is saying is that to an extent—a greater extent than our parents, or even our children, with their mix-and-match lives—all of us in the great white middle class attended the same childhood. Because there were so many middle-class baby-boom kids, because so many of us were born into prosperity (or at least what seemed like a realistic hope for prosperity), and because back then there was so much attention paid to raising kids in a uniform "scientific" way, there was for the first time—beginning with Dr. Spock before we were even born, and continuing till the time we took our SATs with our number 2 pencils—an America-wide, assembly-line homogeneity to our upbringing. This is not to say that we are homogenous now, or that we spend our time reminiscing over Jed Clampitt and Bullwinkle the Moose—but only that from the sheer volume of childhood experience so many of us shared, there emerged an unprecedented generational shorthand.

I recently had dinner with an old friend, a woman two years younger than I am, who a couple of years ago had moved to Texas to live with a man with whom she had fallen in love. The relationship hadn't worked out, but because she had a good job, a nice apartment, and a few friends there, she had stayed on, though she still thinks of New York, where she's spent most of her "adult" life, as home, and talks about returning once she's ready to settle down for good. "I feel that there's a life I'm supposed to have, a life I was raised to have," she said. "And I feel that if I do move back, I'd have to 'find' it fast or else I never will." I asked her what kind of life it was that she was supposed to have, was raised to have. "I don't know anymore," she said. "I can't remember."

That got us talking, and we spent a long time over our Mexican food trying to reconcile the children we had been with the adults we've since become. We weren't surprised that our respective childhoods had so much paraphernalia in common—Tiny Tears dolls, Schwinn bikes, stacks of 45 RPM records. What struck us both, even more than the paraphernalia, was the ineffable certainty we had absorbed from our times that, as my friend put it, "nothing *really* bad could happen." Maybe you'd flunk a test, or miss an important dance— but in the bigger national context, we were so surely on the right moral, economic, technological, and political tracks that it was unimaginable that we could be tempted from our exalted course.

Like America in those days, we had been arrogant, naive, and chaste, all at the same time. We could both recall, for example, the ritual of taking sugar cubes three times so we wouldn't get polio. My friend thought *polio* was a synonym for *disease,* and that the sugar cubes meant she'd never again get sick. She was therefore amazed when, shortly afterward, she'd had to have her tonsils removed; the sugar cubes, she thought, hadn't worked. And we both remembered sitting huddled under our school desks during nuclear-war drills, both of us having reasoned that nuclear war couldn't be much of a threat if our desks could protect us. I was old enough (though she wasn't) to remember Khrushchev banging his shoe on the table at the United Nations; I thought that if he were our enemy, he was a pretty silly guy, not so threatening. Though neither of us was wealthy, as upwardly mobile kids we'd thought that as a matter of course people automatically got richer as they got older, the way wine improves with age. As for sex, we'd seen the same, or similar, slide shows on the subject. "I thought that sex was something beautiful that happened when two anatomical diagrams fell in love," she said. Right. And if my parents fought, I used to think that they were the *only* parents who did. "Yeah," my friend said, "nobody fought next door." (I wonder now: Was the divorce rate so low in the postwar years for the sake of the children, or for the sake of the myth?)

Even our toys expressed the optimism of the postwar years—but, as it would turn out, these toys did not "rehearse" us for adulthood as we would come to know it; instead they prepared us for roles in the myth that would soon be obsolete. Davy Crockett hats, for example, inspired little boys to conquer the frontier—any and all frontiers. (Don't you remember thinking you'd vacation on the moon? And don't you remember believing that all diseases would be eradicated? That technology could solve all our problems?) But now these frontiers were rather more formidable than we'd been told. G.I. Joe taught boys that war was heroic and fun; Vietnam would teach them something else. My friends and I—with our separate toys for girls—all had Barbie and Ken dolls, but all Barbie could do was dress up and Ken, one of the dumbest dolls ever made, couldn't do anything at all; most of us would have to be more resourceful with our lives. Have the skills you learned with your Easy-Bake Oven helped you much? And have you ever been asked in a job interview what color your Mr. Potato Head was?

I know it sounds odd for a grown woman to complain that her Mr. Potato Head let her down and that her childhood in general didn't deliver on its promises, and I don't mean to overdo the point; on the whole, I'm thankful not to be a grown-up Barbie doll. Nevertheless, as one historian of the 1950s put it, "From somewhere deep in the national psychology came the surest affirmation of tomorrow." I doubt that I speak only for myself when I say that as a child I came to believe in this "affirmation of tomorrow"; as a child I truly thought that all of us were experiencing only the beginning of the good times. I had a vision of what this future would be like, a vision my temporarily Texan friend corroborated at dinner that night: It would be the way life was on *The Jetsons*—happy, easy, uncomplicated, prosperous, futuristic. That was the message that came through to me. So I'm not complaining about my toys, really. It's just that when the real future came, it came, to postwar kids and grown-ups alike, as a surprise.

As David Riesman and his collaborators point out in *The Lonely Crowd,* their classic book about the "chang-

ing American character" published in 1950, an imbalance of births and deaths puts inordinate pressure
on a society; if the imbalance is severe enough, the society's traditions no longer hold it together. Never was
this truer than after the War, when so many of us were
born, and the oldest generation then alive began living
much longer. Riesman goes a step further: In a time of
great social or educational mobility, parental and
cultural authority disintegrates. Riesman displayed uncanny foresightedness, for in 1950, the changes he
wrote about had barely begun.

If I had to give an award to the individual who did
the most to change our "national character" after the
War and to weaken the bonds that had held our society
together, without hesitation I'd give it to Bill Levitt,
who in 1949, smack in the middle of some Hicksville,
Long Island, potato fields, far from a town, or public
transportation, or child-care facilities, and *really* far
from any hint of black people, opened Levittown, the
model postwar suburban housing development, a
ready-built community that would soon be imitated all
over the country. When the model house of Levitt's in-
stant development, which was to hold 75,000 people,
first opened, $11 million worth of housing (at $7,990 a
house, no money down) was sold in three and a half
hours. As Dolores Hayden describes Levittown in
Redesigning the American Dream:

> In Hicksville, nothing is on a straight line. Roads curve
> to lead the eye around the corner, but every road is
> lined with identical houses. There is no industry in
> Hicksville except the construction industry. Each new
> Cape Cod house is designed to be a self-contained

world, with white picket fence, green lawn, living room with television set built into the wall, kitchen with Bendix washing machine built into the laundry alcove. Every family is expected to consist of male breadwinner, female housewife, and their children.

Levitt had his Utopia all figured out, down to its politics: "No man who owns his own house and lot can be a Communist," he said. "He has too much to do."

Levitt, and those all over the country who copied him, did as much to change the national character as they did to change the national landscape. Three-quarters of the total housing in this country has been built since 1940. In 1950, the suburban population was 36 million; by 1970 it had doubled. During the 1950s, the population in the suburbs grew by some 83 percent. According to the media, and increasingly in fact, the suburbs—and, more important, the packaged suburban life that by now needs no description—became the prevailing way of life in America.

Not only were the suburbs designed in a conformist spirit and around the "togetherness" myth, but these communities were also brand-new, without the kinds of family and social bonds that traditionally held networks of people together. What's more, it wasn't going to be easy to nurture lasting community bonds within these interchangeable suburbs: By 1960, for various reasons (including the new practice of corporate transferring, upwardly mobile suburb-hopping, and the inevitable decline of urban life, with all the building energy concentrated outside city limits), one out of every five people in America was moving *every year*. Living, as so many of us were, in communities far from our extended families, with no permanent roots, in pristine developments without history or rituals of their own, for many of us, the hometown America and the social solidarity that Riesman wrote about existed only in our imaginations.

Although the suburbs have taken enough of a beating (and triumphed, as many second-generation suburbanites will be happy to testify), their role in Riesman's formula is indisputable, for without a tidal wave of children—Riesman's imbalance of births and deaths—the suburbs would never have made functional sense. What's more, without that same tidal wave of children, along with the concurrent educational and social mobility of the postwar years, the parental and cultural dissolution that Riesman worried about would never have caused such shattering reverberations fifteen years or so after Levitt opened his Levittown, when the well-modulated voice of cultural authority couldn't be heard over the children's voices as they marched, rioted, and protested to the music of the sixties.

As to educational mobility: 85 percent of those born between 1947 and 1951 would graduate from high school; only 35 percent of their parents had. Whatever else can be said about it, education broadens one's world. Regardless of whether your parents happened to have been well educated, and forgetting about the deficiencies in the average postwar public education, there was an education gap that separated postwar kids from their elders. Beyond the three Rs, many of us were exposed to music and dance lessons, travel, and other extracurricular experiences that weren't so readily available to our parents during the hard years of the Depression. And, as we've seen, baby-boom kids

were the "starting over" generation. Our parents still
had the memories of their generation to contend with.

There were other odd factors that separated kids
from grown-ups back then, too, factors that very likely
no one thought about at the time—call them the curiosities of postwar youth. For one thing, not only did
postwar families have more children on the average
than the generations immediately preceding them, but
the children were also spaced more closely together
(the ideal was thought to be thirteen months apart, so
that the mothers could get diapers "over with"), as
they had not always been in the past. Thus in par-
ent/children feuds, and in a permissive time, the kids
had more leverage in their own families than their parents had had when they were growing up. Postwar kids
were bigger than their parents, too—not only bigger,
but we grew bigger faster: Fifty years ago, adults didn't
achieve full stature until they were twenty-nine or so.
Today, girls reach full height at seventeen, boys at
nineteen. And the age at which we reach puberty has
been going down steadily for more than a century.

So there we were, for starters, hulking, sex-starved,
precociously educated children, outnumbering the
grown-ups by a lot, many of us living in communities
that offered us little sense of our ties to our history,
and facing a future that, as time went on, looked less
and less optimistic. In the understated words of an
early SDS manifesto, which appeared just as the first
baby-boom "children" were applying to college, "We
are people of this generation, bred in at least modest
comfort, housed now in universities, looking uncom-
fortably forward to the world we inherit."

No wonder, as Riesman had predicted, and as the

promises of peace and prosperity were broken one by one, that parental and cultural bonds began to fray. Postwar parents—who, as we've seen, were occupied with their own middle-aged problems and expectations—had no choice but to let their children go and, in good faith, leave us to the mercy of our culture. The problem, of course, was that there was no longer a culture to leave us to, and so what our parents unwittingly did was to leave us to ourselves.

When I think of Riesman's elusive cultural bonds, I can't help being reminded of a terrifying film I had to see over and over in psychology classes in both high school and college. It was the film that showed that monkeys nurtured by surrogate mothers made of terrycloth fared much better than monkeys forced to cling to mothers made of wire and who ended up more or less catatonic. Our culture, the myth that carried us through the fifties and early sixties, which had seemed so secure, so comforting at the time, had turned out in fact to be the wire-monkey mother.

By the time we postwar kids were ready to leave home and in the absence of anything better, or anything else, youth—as a way of life, as a belief system, as a community, setting up traditions of its own—became the refuge, the religion of the young.

| 5 |

A QUESTION OF BALANCE

When I was about twenty, at college during the early seventies, I had a friend called Roger. I've forgotten his last name—it began with a *D*—and I don't know exactly how I met him; in those more trusting days people often just turned up in your life, or you might even find them sleeping on your floor. Roger was hard-living and disorganized, but winning, in that energetic but unfocused way of bright and decent people who don't count discipline among their virtues. He had a habit of calling up at odd hours of the night and asking me to come over. He was a "mess," he would explain, and he needed company. I was always puzzled by these requests, because I didn't know him well, and he had plenty of other friends to whom he was closer, but we developed a bizarre, platonic affection. I don't know why he chose to call me, but for my part, I liked feeling needed, like a nurse on call. Also, since Roger was pretty wild then and I wasn't, there was a vicarious thrill for me in watching one of his evenings wind down and a genuine relief in knowing that Roger, who was really very sweet, had made it through another night. So when he'd call, I'd throw on my jeans and— without a thought to safety or the late hour (unimaginable to me now)—head out into the night.

Sometimes I'd get to Roger's to find a party going on, so I'd leave, though not offended that I hadn't been invited. It would have been a party that had just evolved, not something you'd be invited to, and I could easily have joined it if I'd wanted to. Other times he'd be asleep by the time I arrived, and I'd turn off the lights for him, lock the door behind me, and go home, by then a little restless.

Most times, though, Roger would be pacing. He had the face of a nine-year-old choirboy and a body like John Belushi's; in his agitation he appeared very strong. I mostly remember him wearing a faded blue terrycloth bathrobe over his jeans and a gray T-shirt, barefoot, storming around his apartment. He had three or four TV sets and they'd all be on, tuned to different channels, with the volume off. Beer cans, packs of rolling papers, a hash pipe, overflowing ashtrays, and record albums strewn about explained his condition. While he paced, he talked, not to me, really, but he talked nonstop, thrusting his arms this way and that, by turns angry, sad, troubled, or just out of it. I didn't really have to listen; I already knew what Roger's problems were, because back then my friends and I all had the same "problems," more or less.

I don't know much about how college kids feel these

days; it's said that they look to Wall Street and not to Siddhartha, as I did, to find the meaning of life, but maybe it's not fair to generalize. Besides, they've a clear idea (we all do now) that adulthood brings with it no guarantees. At Roger's apartment, though, things were different. I knew, Roger knew, everybody knew, that times were bad for the American Dream as I had known it. I knew I would never again live the safe, tidy life my parents had built for their family after the Second World War. But that's all I knew. The more I listened to the "interpreters" of the time—Gloria Steinem, Ralph Nader, the Berrigans, Bob Dylan, Daniel Ellsberg, Timothy Leary—the more confused I felt; it would take a long time to sort out the violence, the pain, the disconnectedness of those years. Senseless as it may sound now, Roger's apartment seemed to me as tranquil a place as any in the meantime. I liked being there, and when, hours later, I'd go home, I always felt calm and refreshed, for reasons I never quite understood.

One night, as I was leaving, a middle-aged man was walking through Roger's courtyard, going home himself, I suppose. "Damn hippies," he cursed with real venom, and I looked around for the damn hippies, but, as you might expect, there was no one there but me.

hip·pie (hip/e), *n.* a person, esp. of the late 1960s, who rejects established institutions and values and seeks spontaneity, direct personal relations expressing love, and expanded consciousness, most obviously expressed by wearing unconventional costumes ornamented with flowers, beads, and bells, and by taking psychedelic drugs.

Hippie. Somehow this doesn't look right, even though it's straight out of the dictionary. I'm relieved to say I was never the flower or bell-ornament type, but I did have a great fringed suede vest with red and yellow wooden beads on it. Not that *hippie* was a word that sounded real even then; it was one of those words (like *yippies* and *yuppies*) meant for the media, not for actual people. Around my parents I might have claimed to be a hippie, as a concise way to let them know that I was on the "other side," but my friends and I would never have called one another hippies. Hippies weren't cool, and we didn't like labels. And these memories of mine aren't even, technically, from the sixties; until 1969, all I wanted to be was a high school cheerleader, not a radical. Such as they were, my sixties took place in the seventies.

I can't speak for everyone, but I know I wasn't looking for spontaneity in my Roger days; I was looking for order. To "seek spontaneity" is a contradiction. Spontaneity just happens. You can't go looking for it, though I know plenty of people who've tried. If expanded consciousness was a concern, it was because the consciousness I had grown up with was no longer pertinent or enough. There was the personal sense of loss I felt; my parents weren't married anymore, and I had no real "home" to go back to. But more than that, the larger world was harder-edged: It seemed that no one had a home to go back to anymore—and in the chaos of those days, Roger's apartment, with its black-lit posters falling down, its lava lamp to stare at, and its ragged American flag draped over a sofa, seemed to me like a kind of chapel, the only place where I felt at home.

*   *   *

The sixties started in the summer of 1985 for two teenagers I know when they discovered the music of Crosby, Stills, and Nash. Their father and stepmother, close friends of mine, were amused at first, certain that this phase would pass quickly. But no. By the next summer, the kids were also listening to the Grateful Dead and the Moody Blues, burning incense, and watching *Woodstock* and *Easy Rider* on the VCR; one of them had a poster of the long-dead Jimi Hendrix tacked to a wall. The younger kid, in a burst of entre-preneurial fervor, did a brisk business for a while sell-ing tie-dyed T-shirts, and when I was examining his still-damp stock one day, I asked him how his summer was going. "Okay, I guess," he said. "I'm doing a lot of thinking." He was thinking about South Africa, Amer-ica's homeless, President Reagan's bombing of Libya earlier that spring, terrorism, and, not incidentally, where, with college only a semester away, his own life was headed. As I negotiated to buy a shirt (a good chunk of his brisk business came from selling shirts to grown-ups) and heard strains of Grace Slick singing "White Rabbit" in the background, I felt as over-whelmed and hopeful and sad as I had felt lost in my own "sixties," trying to come to terms with a time that made no sense.

As the second summer of the teenagers' sixties re-vival progressed, their father and stepmother began to complain: Why, they wondered, were these kids trying to pilfer an older generation's history? What did they know of the ugliness of Vietnam, the struggles for civil rights, women's liberation, and the rest of it? Why couldn't they start a youth movement of their own? Be-

sides, my friends admitted, it made them uncomfortable to be immersed again in the emotional turbulence
of the sixties: "This just brings it all back," they said.

Brings what back? The War, bra-burnings, sit-ins, the
Smothers Brothers? I doubt that's the problem. Instead,
I suspect my friends were thinking back to (and trying to
spare the kids from) the private, lonely anguish so many
of us felt during and after the sixties, when all of America's inalienable support systems—our belief in monog-
amy, marriage, family, the government, our jobs, our
future, our values, our selves—seemed to be crumbling.
And no single generation can claim that anguish as entirely its own.

When I think of my sixties, I think of Roger during
the seventies, and of how I was trying to find my way
for some years after that—long after I'd come of age
by any conventional definition. A younger friend remembers his sixties as beginning "in 1979, I guess,
when I first smoked a lot of dope, freshman year. It *felt*
like the sixties—for a while we were questioning everything." A woman I know was a housewife with two kids
throughout the real sixties; she's the only person I've
ever met who attended the March on Washington in
1963, where Martin Luther King gave his "I Have a
Dream" speech. Now a divorced and remarried working woman in her fifties, she remembers the March as
the single most important event that "snapped" her out
of her old life, which she won't explain, except to say
that it was "mindless and sad." The most zealous pro-
tester I know from those years is a woman who used to
leave her Park Avenue apartment most mornings during the late sixties in jeans, her baby strapped somehow
to her hip, and take a cab to Wall Street, where she

solicited signatures for petitions and joined one of the protests held almost daily, all the while dodging her husband's friends and colleagues, and, as she might have put it then, looking for herself. At night she'd go home to Park Avenue. If you'd known her in the sixties, you wouldn't recognize her as the direct and self-reliant woman she has since become. And I remember once running into the father of a high school friend of mine whom I hadn't seen in months—this must have been about 1970. I was touched to see that he had grown a set of discreet sideburns, as if his new hairstyle would say for him what he couldn't or didn't dare say for himself. Though I hadn't liked him before, I did now.

In our apprehension, and regardless of age, we were as united as we were divided, all of us looking for something to believe in. What set my generation (give or take) apart was our intuition, as young people on the cusp of adulthood, that not only had we lost the world we'd come from, but that no new world had taken shape for us to grow up into. Faced with this dilemma, we did what history tells us young people in precarious straits have always done: We turned to religion. We converted.

I remember going to church once during my Roger days, when I was visiting a friend's family over a long weekend. The church was Unitarian, I think, and the service amazed me—I hadn't been to church in a long time. The minister was wearing the requisite robe, but his hair covered his ears and he peered out at his congregation through granny glasses; he seemed to be having fun. The subject for the sermon was something

like "Is War Ever Okay?" and during the usual pauses
for hymns and the collection, a guitarist sang antiwar
songs into the microphone: "How many deaths will it
take till he knows / That too many people have died?"
There was no communion offered that day, but it
would have seemed more in keeping with the tone of
the service for the minister to call his congregation up
row by row to share a joint than to offer them a wafer
and grape juice. He must have reasoned that if people
wouldn't go to church in the sixties, why not bring the
sixties to the church?

Church attendance in America began to decline
(eventually by 10 percent) in the late fifties, which is
understandable, for the spirit of the sixties, a time in
which anyone of any age could come of age all over
again, was itself a religion, and you didn't have to go to
church to practice it. Beginning in the sixties—with
marriages, families, communities, the stable postwar
way of life at risk; in a country at war, with the political
and economic future, strained by Vietnam, beginning
to look bleak—the sixties offered what any fledgling
religion does: a way to shake off an old world and join
a new one.

"My age is thirty-three," Abbie Hoffman testified at
the Chicago Seven conspiracy trial in 1969. "I am a
child of the sixties." (To be a child of the sixties was to
be reborn—but, as Hoffman said, as a child. No one
ever said, "I am a grown-up of the sixties.") His state-
ment was tantamount to saying, "I'm a Presbyterian,"
or, "I'm Jewish." It was a calling card, a credential; he
was one of the flock. And to be a child of the sixties
was, in the words of the "Woodstock" song, to "set"
one's "soul free," to be a "child of God," to get "back to
the garden," just like in Genesis.

What is more, you could become a church member even if you left your soul right where it was. I'd never thought of myself as a devout child of the sixties—I'd thought the real sixties kids lived in Haight-Ashbury, had stringy hair and out-of-wedlock kids named Sunshine and Etherea. It wasn't till much later that I saw just how much of the sixties message I'd absorbed without even knowing it.

Think of the way many religions govern the appearance of their followers—Orthodox Jews with their tendril side curls and yarmulkes, the saffron robes of the Hare Krishnas, or the pastel outfits of Episcopalian Sunday golfers. The costumes of the sixties also denoted religion: long hair, bell-bottom jeans, peasant clothing, tie-dyed shirts, and so on. You could tell a "child of the sixties" from afar (even if you couldn't, owing to length of hair, tell the sex of that child). A simple pair of jeans, styled, frayed, faded, and fitted just so, could say it all: I am against the War; I am for civil rights; my values are not corrupt; I'm a believer.

Religions also control marital, sexual, and contraceptive behavior; take the Bible's warnings against masturbation and fooling around with neighbors' spouses, and its reminders about "multiplying." The sixties had a sexual doctrine, too: free love, open sexuality, the abolition of many sexual taboos, and all the masturbation you wanted with no guilt. Contraceptives were in; multiplying was out (remember Zero Population Growth?). And where women a generation older than I were afraid of losing their virginity, many women my age were embarrassed to have kept theirs too long.

Christmas carols are played over the radio during the season—but sixties music has played all year long for decades; it never goes out of season: Three Dog

Night's "Joy to the World," "Stairway to Heaven," "One toke over the line, sweet Jesus." There were promises of enlightenment in the hymns, peace, good times, solidarity, a new age dawning (Aquarius), even perennial youth ("What a drag it is getting old"). How we looked for messages in the music, even going so far as to play the records backward to look for hidden bits of truth!

Pilgrimages? Monterey, the disastrous Altamont, the marches, be-ins, sit-ins. Ceremonies? Write-your-own nuptials held at the edges of creeks. Rituals? Not the sign of the cross, but the peace sign; holy water to fill up waterpipes; you broke bread together by passing a joint to your neighbor. Scriptures? *Rolling Stone, Why Are We in Vietnam?, The Whole Earth Catalog, The Electric Kool-Aid Acid Test, The Medium Is the Message, Slaughterhouse-Five.* Password? Relevant. Transcendental experiences? Acid. Martyrs? Kent State. The persecuted? Soldiers fighting in Vietnam, blacks, women, students. The persecutors? Corporations destroying souls, Agent Orange, Kissinger and Nixon and their friends—the grown-ups who had corrupted the system and the society.

In addition, like any good religion, the sixties even had its own taboo: the ostentatious pursuit, discussion, or display of money.

Among the people I know, there seems to be a split—on the one hand, those who remember their sixties fondly and, on the other, those who'd rather not talk about it at all. "I'm getting fat, I'm almost forty, and I have no money," replied a friend, when I asked if he wanted to talk about it. "Do we have to?" But another friend has particularly happy memories of living (emphasis on living) in Vermont during her stretched-out college years. "There *was* a lot of love," she says. To the question "How did you live?" she answers by talking about where she lived, whom she lived with, what their lives were like. "But how did you live?" I asked again (emphasis on how). "What about money?"

"Money wasn't important then. It really wasn't. Nobody had any and it didn't matter."

Somebody must have had some money, at least. "Well, yeah, you always had enough to get by."

But where did you get it? Where did it come from? "I don't know. It wasn't a lot; there was just enough."

Did you get it from your parents? "I don't know. I guess so."

As for the creed, there were posters to spell out the rules: You do your thing and I'll do mine; march to the beat of your own drummer; don't trust the establishment or join it. For all the talk about getting the "people" together, this creed, it seems to me in retrospect, was a lonely one. I haven't seen a copy of "Desiderata" in years, but I still remember how solemn its message seemed, Scotch-taped to a closet door I once had: I wasn't put in this world to live to your expectations, nor you to mine. But the poster was wrong. Isn't the point that we're all of us here to live up to one another's expectations? And if we're all doing our own things, that's not getting the people together to set up a new world. Instead, that's the behavior you'd expect during free time in a nursery school. The problem with this creed was that it offered no lucid plan for setting up one's life in the real world. Above all, to be a child of the sixties was to be a child: There was no provision for an afterlife.

Most of us were not wholehearted activists in the sixties (or ever), or fanatics, or heroes, but simply "kids in jeans," as a friend of mine puts it. I have to remind myself sometimes how it really was—and it wasn't all selfless giving of oneself to causes, or it wasn't for me, anyway. I am the sort who when asked to attend a peace rally (or nuclear rally or pro-choice rally) will not automatically say, "Yes, of course," but will temporize. Out of shameful laziness and an aversion to crowds and hassles, I will ask instead what time the rally is and what the weather is supposed to be like, before consulting my calendar and conscience. If in those years I stood up to be counted at all, I was just one of those millions of "kids in jeans," hiding behind my youth, like a mask.

The narrator of Kurt Vonnegut's *Galápagos*, looking back on our time a million years from now, observes: "Back when childhoods were often so protracted, it is unsurprising that so many people got into the lifelong habit of believing, even after their parents were gone, that somebody was always watching over them—God or a saint or a guardian angel or the stars or whatever." That was part of what it meant to be a child of the sixties: that no matter what, you'd be saved, if for no other reason than that you believed in the right things. Nice kids in jeans were good guys; things would work out in one way or another.

I doubt that soldiers in combat in Vietnam, or poor or working-class kids whose childhoods were not "protracted," could have felt cosmically protected from unknown dangers in the way Vonnegut describes, but throughout the college years of the postwar generation, when a higher percentage of America's young people than ever before were in college, it is easy to understand how so many kids could have come to believe in a guardian angel, or the stars, or whatever. For one thing, a college degree in this country had always automatically promised the good life, as if the degree itself were a guardian angel. In the sixties, 20 percent of college-age kids were in college (compared with 9 percent in the forties and fifties); by 1981, 35 percent were in college. Among baby-boom college graduates today, two-thirds of their fathers had, by contrast, no higher education at all.

Naturally it was easy for baby-boom college kids to rebel against the good life. A good many of us, growing up as we had in the prosperous fifties and sixties, had always known relative comfort and security and, as students, felt that we could call the good life up again at will; didn't our degrees entitle us to it?

Even the majority of us, the weekend rebels who never got arrested, never moved to teepees or communes, and who (secretly) found at least a few things in the "establishment" to admire, believed that we wouldn't end up entirely on our own. For all our fitful questioning, for all the fights between generations, for all the complaints against society, it was still easy deep down to feel certain that the "culture" that had always provided for us so magnanimously would continue to do so. Under the nervous surface of the times, many sixties kids of all ages believed what the children in *Peter Pan* did: "Off we skip like the most heartless things in the world, which is what children are, but so attractive; and then when we have need of special attention we nobly return for it, confident that we will be embraced instead of smacked." We believed that our parents, our culture, our country would take us back. As long as you could believe in a guardian angel, the stars, or your college degree, you could remain a sixties child.

The postwar young had mastered youth in a way no other generation in our history ever had. Where earlier generations had rushed their youth along (to get away from home, make their own decisions, buy six-packs, dance close together, wear grown-up clothes, have sex), we wanted to stretch ours out. We were already away from home, often with checks coming in once a month, having sex, dancing any way we wanted, choosing our clothes, drinking, and doing drugs besides. Moreover, we were envied by the older generations: We weren't imitating them; they were imitating us. In 1971, more than two million people bought *The Greening of America,* in which a professor at Yale described in awe what he'd learned from his students! To be touched by youth was to be blessed, and nobody could express youth the way children of the sixties could.

Other things kept us young as well. Beginning in the seventies, there weren't enough jobs or houses to accommodate us all as grown-ups; we were a big generation, heavy on college graduates and intent that our jobs should be "meaningful," entering a shrinking job market. How much easier therefore to stay young, go back to school, get a job "for now," move back in with one's parents, or just float for a while. Things would always work out, one way or another. Nothing really bad could happen—and for many of us, nothing really bad *has* happened.

Nevertheless, even the most devout children of the sixties could tell when the religion stopped working. Like the kids in *Peter Pan,* most of us returned when we needed special attention, and were confident that we'd be embraced instead of smacked. Sooner or later, it was time to get out and join the world; we began to get on with our grown-up lives.

For many of us, however, at least for many of the people I know, what remains from our sixties is a lingering self-consciousness in the way we express ourselves as adults that wasn't there when we were expressing ourselves as kids—a resistance to feeling like a "real" grown-up, as if real grown-ups were still the enemy, or as if our fate were still entirely in the hands of an older generation and guardian angels and the stars. It's right for children to feel powerless, and blameless, in this way, but when adults feel powerless, they *are* powerless. They're also cheating—cheating themselves mostly—and missing out on the special pleasures of adulthood that children can never know.

I believe there is an intuition with which the adult approaches the world that is different from a child's. Imagine, for example, a father who takes his young son to visit an ailing wheelchair-bound great-uncle in a nursing home. The child will see an ailing old man in a wheelchair; he'll probably be frightened, but he won't know why. The father, however, if he's an adult, sees something different. He will see someone who is probably close to death, who has lived his life, has loved, worked, maybe watched children grow up, hung curtains, had pretty things, seen other people die. The father might remember his uncle when he was vigorous and know, too, that his uncle remembers him as a child. The father knows that he is visiting his uncle but also that he is visiting time, watching a preview of his own life, and his son's. He knows that there's a sadness to this, but also an inevitability to it; he'll be a richer man for having learned the lesson. The child sees none of this, and that's why he's restless, and afraid. You might ask yourself: Are you the child here, or the father?

In a poem called "The Young Man's Song," Yeats was writing about falling in love, but could as easily have been writing about accepting life itself:

> *I whispered, "I am too young,"*
> *And then, "I am old enough;" . . .*
> *One cannot begin it too soon.*

| 6 |

CALLING CARD

The employment agency took its name from a famous university and promised in its ad that it specialized in publishing jobs for college graduates. I thought I was a shoo-in. Not only was I a college graduate; I also had a brand-new master's degree in English. It was July in New York, and first thing on a hot Monday morning I joined the working world on the subway, wearing my black-and-white-checked "interview dress," which felt sticky and too formal; I wasn't used to dressing up. It was 1973, and I was twenty-two.

The agency was on a high-up floor in a dingy office building near Grand Central Station. When I arrived, I approached the guard for directions; he rolled his eyes and gestured toward an elevator bank, where a dozen or so young people had gathered. They were as dressed up as I was—career people, I thought, and I felt surprisingly eager, excited actually, at the thought

of joining them. I had a vague idea that the right job
could bring out a vibrant, confident, attractive new me:
Suddenly I could imagine myself, briefcase in hand,
striding purposefully into my office each morning,
glancing at my watch and greeting my colleagues, the
way Faye Dunaway might do it. I would carry my
power well and use it kindly. I would wear high heels
without tripping.

When we got in the elevator, one of the young men
pressed the button indicating the same floor I was
going to. Two other people pressed different buttons,
but the rest of us, as it turned out, were going not only
to the same floor but also to the same agency. All at
once, I knew that these people were not my future colleagues. They were my competition.

When we reached our floor, after a long, mostly silent ride, we all piled out of the elevator, looked
around for the suite number the ad had given, then
walked toward it *en masse*, passing a disorderly queue
of more young people leaning or sitting against the
wall, carrying the employment section of the Sunday
paper, résumés, and the rest of their job-hunting
equipment. Someone had brought a radio, so there was
rock music playing in the hallway. A woman in a pink
dress was sitting on a spread-out beach towel. When we
got to the door of the agency, another young woman at
the head of the line explained everything: "There's the
line," she said, pointing back the way we'd come. We
retraced our steps toward the elevator and sat down
against the wall. It was now ten minutes past ten; the
agency had opened at nine-thirty.

Clearly some of the others in the line were savvier
about job hunting than I was: The veterans not only

had résumés and the want-ad section in hand, but also cups of coffee and Danish, enough books or magazines to fill up a day, and candy bars; I was grateful for the sound of the radio. Once in a while, the door of the agency opened to allow one person to leave and another to enter. Anxiously, we all studied the one coming out, the way you watch someone leaving a dentist's office as you're dreading your turn.

"What kind of job do you want?" I asked someone from my elevator ride. "I'm going into marketing," he said. "Publishing," I answered, when he asked me the same question. "They specialize in publishing jobs here," I added, pointing to my newspaper. "They specialize in marketing, too," he said, pointing to his. He had been looking for jobs under *M* for marketing and I under *P* for publishing; the agency had run its ad twice—at least twice. Most likely an aspiring trapeze artist would have found under *T* that this agency also specialized in jobs for trapeze artists. After a while, he went for coffee and I held his place in line.

I waited more than two hours; by then the line behind me was longer than it had been when I'd first joined it. Once in a while, someone would announce, "Screw this," and leave before he or she even got inside; jokes trailed up and down the hall. The prevailing spirit was of bored and benign camaraderie. As each of us entered the agency, those behind would call out good luck, but without much hope or heartiness behind it.

Once inside, I straightened my wrinkled dress, prepared to talk about why I wanted to go into publishing and what an asset I'd be to any company. I hoped I would sound impressive. Instead, the receptionist

handed me a clipboard with an application and a pen-
cil on it and told me to sit down and fill it out.

Education: I filled in my degrees.

Previous work experience: Waitressing, odd jobs, things
like that. Nothing to do with publishing. I left the
space blank.

Typing: Yes, I wrote (I had typed all my own papers
in school), though I didn't see how that was pertinent,
not for the likes of Faye Dunaway or me.

I was hungry by the time my name was called. It was
way past lunchtime. I was directed to a cubicle where
my counselor, a woman my age, dressed in jeans, had
my application on her desk. She was eating a sandwich
and bits of lettuce kept falling on my credentials. She
crossed out my master's degree first thing. "Don't talk
about that," she counseled, thereby dismissing the
achievement of which I was most proud. "It'll make
you sound overqualified." I bowed to her expertise and
stared at her corn chips, but she didn't offer me one.

"How fast?" she asked.

"What?"

"Typing. How fast?"

I was sent to take a typing test, and I didn't do very
well. She was discouraged about my prospects in publishing until my typing improved. Still, she had a couple of possibilities, great jobs for me, in fact. She
arranged three "publishing" interviews for me the next
day: one at a textbook publishing company I'd never
heard of two hours away in New Jersey; another as a
reporter for a machinists' newsletter; the third at an
insurance company, writing for its house organ. What
I'd had in mind was more in the line of dark-paneled
walls and glass-enclosed bookcases. "Too bad about
your typing," she said as I left.

I went on those interviews and many more over the next couple of weeks; I also registered with several other agencies that "specialized" in publishing jobs. At all the agencies and on the interviews themselves, I saw the same thing: dozens of young people, inexperienced college graduates just like me, give or take a few I.Q. points and words per minute. For the first time in my life, I understood what it meant to belong to this big, hungry, overqualified generation that had previously seemed only a remote fact of my life. It meant that there might not be enough jobs for all of us, certainly not enough jobs in the field I wanted. It meant that for all I knew about Nathaniel Hawthorne, I couldn't type fast enough. It meant that I wasn't special, or that if I was, it wouldn't be easy to prove it.

Finally I took a job at Montgomery Ward, writing bra and girdle copy for its now-defunct catalogue, a job that my first agency had listed under both "Publishing" and "Marketing," describing it as a glamorous entry-level position in retailing, requiring conceptual and copywriting skills. Faye Dunaway wouldn't have been caught dead in this movie. But it was a job. I had a desk, office supplies, a phone with buttons, and every Friday I got an official-looking paycheck. I went to meetings where I was given stacks of bras and girdles (four- or six-hook closures, reinforced elastic, more or less support) to test my writing skills. On good days I managed to fit all the copy and all the pictures on the same page. On bad days I looked hopelessly at the bras and girdles piled on my desk and couldn't think of one thing to say about them to make them sound worth buying.

Even so, maybe it speaks well for human adaptability that, even on bad days like these, I'd remind myself that the job was a foot in the door, even if it was the wrong door, even if there was reason to worry that I'd never get my foot back *out*. Some people I knew were in worse shape—an English-major friend who knew a lot about Ezra Pound was working as a receptionist for an eye doctor; a musician I knew was working on a tour bus; a would-be teacher I met at about this time was waiting on tables and packing for Alaska, where, he'd heard, teachers were scarce.

Even so, my ambitions and those of my other over-educated (if equally underskilled) friends were, if anything, more intact than they had been before this first sour taste of the real world. Surely we were not cut out for ordinary lives like these. During the (short) time I held my first job, I didn't see myself as someone meant to write bra and girdle copy. That person, that life, didn't count. Like everyone else sitting in the hallway that day, I wanted meaningful work, a vocation—not a spirit-killing job with a pension plan and two weeks paid vacation a year; I'd already seen the damage that could do. The sixties had led me to believe that it was possible, in or out of the system, to be "my own person," and, had I written my own job description, I would have demanded that the position help me find her, and that it pay a good salary for the privilege. What kept me writing bra and girdle copy was my confidence in what I would yet become.

Had I been a man coming of age twenty years before, it's unlikely that I would have had such romantic notions about finding my "calling," finding a job which would reveal heretofore undiscovered meanings in my life. American business at that time was not sympathetic to self-expression, any more than Japanese business, which fills us with nervous contempt at the selfless loyalty it demands from its workers, is today. If I had been a man in my father's generation, I don't doubt that I would have been happy to trade in my serviceman's uniform for another uniform, of gray flannel.

Consider some of the qualities of William H. Whyte Jr.'s "organization man," from the enormously popular book of that title, published in 1956. He (he was never a she) had probably graduated from the service and from either high school or college—college obviously offered him greater corporate opportunities—after World War II; the younger he was, the less intense his residual fear of another Great Depression. He knew that corporations had been expanding: "With so many new departments, divisions, and plants being opened up," Whyte wrote, "many a young man of average ability has been propelled upward so early—and so pleasantly—that he can hardly be blamed if he thinks the momentum is a constant."

By the early fifties, when increasing prosperity in this country was beginning to seem a given, corporate recruiters on college campuses found that their young recruits trusted the onward and upward momentum of the corporate here and now. They didn't ask many questions; they wanted to know what they could do for the corporation to ensure their steady ascent to the top. My friends and I, on the other hand, had graduated not from the army or the navy, but from the sixties. We wanted to know what the system could do for us. Something like what Chrysler would do for Lee Iacocca would have been fine.

What these fifties aspirants were most concerned about instead, recruiters found, was retirement and pension benefits, as though joining a corporation could in itself guarantee them a long and comfortable life. One recruiter interviewed 300 college seniors, none of whom brought up the subject of salary. What these kids were looking for was "security and opportunity" combined, and they believed that they would find them in the anonymity of a large corporation. They believed it enough that they didn't even ask about the salary:

> The premise is, simply, that the goals of the individual and the goals of the organization will work out to be one and the same. The young [organization] men have no cynicism about the "system," and very little skepticism— they don't see it as something to be bucked, but as something to be cooperated with.

The organization wanted its trainees to be extroverted and well adjusted: able to work well within and credit their own ideas to the group; anti-intellectual; willing to allow the organization to decide what was best for them; committed to the corporation for the long haul; conformist in appearance, outside interests, etc.; and not a genius. "We used to look for brilliance," one company president said at the time. "Now . . . we want a well-rounded person who can handle well-rounded people." With corporate America on a roll, its management wanted neither trouble nor innovation. The odds seemed to favor the corporate tortoise over the corporate hare. No sooner had the organization man staked out his office than the dissent against his conformity began; Whyte himself was one of the leading dissenters, and his book became a huge best-seller.

Another popular and extremely influential book published in 1956 was *Growing Up Absurd,* Paul Goodman's stinging attack on the organization man's unexamined life, both in and out of the office:

> People are forced by their better judgment to ask very basic questions: Is it possible, *how* is it possible, to have more meaning and honor in work? to put wealth to some real use? to have a high standard of living of whose quality we are not ashamed? to get social justice for those who have been shamefully left out? to have a use of leisure that is not a dismaying waste of a hundred million adults?

And this was only the beginning. As we'll see, the organization man in America, that symbol of the postwar decade, was as insubstantial as every other myth of those togetherness years—including the stable nuclear family, contented stay-at-home mothers, the promise of ever greater prosperity, and lives that could flourish without pain, self-discovery, or growth. Sooner or later, it was inevitable that Lee Iacocca would quit Ford to do it his way at Chrysler.

Whyte's corporate hero simply could not survive in America. Japanese culture rewards the group player; ours has always exalted the individual—Lee Iacocca, Davy Crockett, Rambo—above all else. Quite apart from any moral reasons for deploring legions of unthinking, unquestioning workers, managers, and executives, the American ethos is deeply individualistic in its very nature. We may not have been born that way, but we were certainly raised that way, and any residual military discipline that kept the organization man in line for a few short postwar years soon declined. For us

to have tried to fashion ourselves to the work ethic that
has proved so congenial—and lucrative—to the Japanese was as unnatural for us as, say, eating Fig New-
tons with chopsticks. In my family there's a legend that
my father was once fired from a corporate job for refusing to wear a hat. Whether the story is true, or
whether he was insubordinate in other ways as well, he
was proud of it; the legend asserted his individuality
for a long time and through many other corporate
jobs. A Japanese worker might be ashamed of the episode, but my father, for all his corporate zeal, needed
to feel separate to feel alive.

Hats or no hats, help was soon on the way for the
organization man. One remedy, as Barbara Ehrenreich
points out in *The Hearts of Men,* was the far-reaching
influence of *Playboy,* which was first published in 1953:
What appeared to be a sex magazine was just as much
a critique of "the gray miasma of conformity" that was
reducing real men to clones in the office (and husband-
clones at home). Whether you read the magazine or
not, its taunting reminder was clear: American men
had choices. Rules in America are made to be broken.

What's more, the latest medical evidence seemed to
substantiate *Playboy's* go-for-the-good-times imperative:
The corporate male, it was "discovered," was subject to
heart disease, stress-related illnesses, and Type-A behavior that would transport him from success to an
early grave. In 1963, Betty Friedan told the other side
of the story in *The Feminine Mystique:* The lot of the
corporate wife was no more, and maybe less, rewarding than that of her husband. And without a corporate
wife behind him, the organization man couldn't
amount to much; she was essential to the package.

Then came the relentless questions of the sixties: Am I all I can be? Am I my own best friend? Am I happy? It was no longer enough to be dutiful. By doing whatever they could (switching from gray suits to blue ones, or from golf to tennis, by deserting wives and children, or staging a mid-life crisis), organization men by the thousands sought to disown the label and reclaim their souls.

The fallout has expressed itself in many ways: to name a few, the end of the breadwinner ethic and a shift in gender roles; the tragedy of untrained women left alone and children left unsupported; the likely impact of this revolt on our well-documented declining productivity; and a turnaround in our belief that what's good for General Motors is necessarily good for the country. We're still looking for "security and opportunity," and we've not escaped bureaucracies— most of us still work for them—but from the perspective of an age when it's every man and woman for him or herself, the organization man, as Whyte described him, was yet another American experiment in self-deception from the fifties that failed.

While attitudes are never easy to measure or prove, I have yet to meet the man or woman today who would agree that his or her goals automatically align with those of the corporation, nor have I met too many people these days who would neglect to ask about the salary before taking a job. To the organization man, one corporation or position was virtually indistinguishable from another, but I don't think that's true today. The discovery that the organization man left behind is this: You're not supposed to lose yourself in your job— you're supposed to find yourself.

*   *   *

When I dreamt of "going into publishing," I was dreaming about a life, not about a living. I believed that "publishing" would be my calling, like medicine or the priesthood. I imagined a Vaseline-lens life in publishing, with carpeted libraries and well-bound books, serious and witty companions, writers discussing the fine points of the latest novel. My work (and on this point I was less clear, since I hadn't a clue what publishers actually *did*) would be valuable and fulfilling. It would give me purpose; it would shape my life. I now realize, with more than a little embarrassment, that that was a lot to ask from an entry-level job in book publishing.

Whatever the calling—publishing, law, medicine, science, social work, or, for my companion in the hallway of the agency, marketing—any such dream promises you a ready-built world to belong to and, at the same time, a way to transcend that world; again, the way Iacocca has done. As a recent survey on American life puts it, "In the strongest sense of a 'calling,' work constitutes a practical ideal of activity and character that makes a person's work morally inseparable from his or her life." (And it isn't just a question of morality: Don't think for a minute that Iacocca's dream is furnished from the secondhand store.)

For my generation, the generation that came of age in the backlash against the organization ethic, the compulsion to define ourselves, even enlarge ourselves through work was a strong one—and much harder to achieve than I imagined it would be when I blithely set my sights on a publishing career in 1973.

In the first place, increases in the Gross National Product had begun to slow down after 1969, a year of recession and the year the oldest of the baby-boom generation turned twenty-three. In 1973, the year I took my typing test, the term "stagflation" first turned up in the papers. Since then, in the words of one of the many studies with the same message, and despite ups and downs in the stock market: "Most Americans over the past decade have faced a sharp slowing down, if not a virtual cessation, of growth in incomes. This represents a significant break with their previous experience and with the expectations encouraged by the unprecedented prosperity of the 1960s." In other words, and as I soon discovered, callings are fine, but a person still needs to eat and pay rent, and, by 1973, rents were rising sharply. As for my library of leather-bound books, well, there's something to be said for paperbacks. By the time my generation, with its sixties-inspired dreams of spiritually fulfilling careers, went to work, the American living standard had begun what seemed likely to be a very long decline.

To make matters worse, because the postwar generation was so damned big, and because of its unprecedented percentage of college graduates with overblown expectations, there were more of us than ever before who were looking not just for a job but for *the* job, while the surplus jobs existed only in low-paying service areas—working at McDonald's, for example. *Forty percent of workers with college degrees were considered overqualified for the jobs they were actually doing in 1976,* and think how much harder it was for workers without degrees. When I finally did get my legitimate job in publishing, I was hired as a secretary—though we were called "assistants" and no one without a degree would have been considered for the job. I was thrilled.

As a generation facing adulthood, moreover, we

were rootless and in critical need of the kind of identity we hoped careers might offer. Many of us did not have close families or hometowns (or any of the other identifying connections our parents or theirs had had); many of us had little reason even to settle in a particular place. We began to marry later and thus did not establish family ties of our own early on. In the lonely cities and towns to which we began to migrate for work, the job—once you found it—could easily become more or less your entire life, especially since you knew that if you didn't want to work weekends, someone else did.

On the other hand, the compulsion to find a calling and not just a job brings with it a freedom and a willingness to take risks—risks that the organization man, with his pension and benefits all lined up, found comforting to forgo. "I don't know; it was just wrong. So I left," says a friend, describing his unplanned departure from a secure job he once held. Now he shakes his head at his foolhardiness—but he never regretted his decision. Besides, it's easier to maneuver among ladders of success when you're only a rung or two up, when you haven't yet established permanent ties of your own, and when there's the chance that you'll gain more than you'll lose from taking a risk.

"It now takes another decade to grow up in our culture," one analyst of the "postponed generation" complains. "Middle-class Americans used to do it in their early twenties. It now seems to happen on either side of thirty." Ironically, however, the earlier generation to whom the analyst compares us is, of course, the anomalous generation of organization men who took their corporate vows without questioning them, only to regret it later.

*   *   *

I was lucky. I found a good facsimile of the job I had
dreamed of in publishing and worked at it for nine
years, made some lasting friends, and did well; I grew
a lot in my job and learned some things about the
world and myself that I wouldn't have learned otherwise. Yet over time, my job, even though it offered
more sustenance to the mind and spirit than many jobs
do, and was heaven compared to describing cut-rate
bras and girdles, began to give way to still other
dreams. I caught myself looking out my office window
more than I should have; I had learned what a "calling" can and cannot do.

One problem was learning that behind every calling
there's a job. What I never imagined in my dreams
were endless piles of papers and memos, office politics,
difficult colleagues—the stuff of which real jobs are
made. I had had no idea how difficult it is to have a
voice in a bureaucracy, and how hollow the identity
payoff can seem after you've put in your time. My job
wasn't "me" anymore.

A woman I know, a successful interior designer, explains it: "I absolutely love designing rooms. It's like:
I'm there in every room I do. The problem is the people who live in them." In her case, time and again she
interprets for her clients what they claim to want in a
room, only to find out that they don't know what they
want at all. Or: "This is sort of my dream," the owner
of a popular restaurant in New York told me. "I always
loved the idea of seeing people having a nice time in a
pretty place, enjoying the food I've created for them.
But people do things—someone ordered chanterelles,
then was upset because he didn't like mushrooms. You

want people to say thank you, not just pay their checks." Even so, something keeps this designer designing, the chef serving mushrooms, and others reconciling their dreams with what they do, at least for now. But I had to go on. Maybe I felt out of touch with what William James calls the "moving present"; or maybe something else was wrong.

"What's wrong with my job is that I don't have a girlfriend," a friend told me the other night at dinner. And there's another problem with putting all your hopes for finding an identity into a calling. No matter how great, or how terrible, your career is, a career by itself is never a life.

| 7 |

IDENTITY

A couple of years ago, I received a letter from the "girl" who had been my best friend during the seventh and eighth grades when I lived outside of Cleveland. There were several reasons why I had felt lucky to be her best friend. For one thing, her hair could be made to curl into the perfect flip, whereas mine never could. She also had robust, air-clearing fights with her mother, which neither my mother nor I would have been capable of. I envied the abandon of these wonderful quarrels. She also never worried about her grades the way I did and was a good student anyway.

I had moved away to suburban Chicago by the ninth grade, so we weren't best friends anymore, but for a while we kept in touch regularly, through gushy schoolgirl letters and, on special occasions, long-distance calls. The letters dropped off over the years, but we did meet once again in New York, when I was in graduate school and she was working at a travel agency. After that, we lost track of each other, until about ten years later when this letter, which she had gone to some trouble to send, in care of the publisher of my first book, arrived in my mailbox. As usual, her letter—this one with an unfamiliar Pacific Northwest postmark—was full of news.

She wrote that her daughter (daughter? what daughter?) was now in the first grade, and that her husband (husband?) had divorced her, which, in time, had been fine with her, all for the best, really. She had stayed in the house (house?) and somehow had managed to keep it going, working here and there, but nothing serious, no real career, though she was thinking seriously about that now. She was writing the letter as she waited for the washing-machine repairman (washing machine?), who was coming yet again to fix what she thought must be the oldest washing machine still in operation west of the Mississippi. Her mother had seen me on a TV show promoting my book—that's how she had found me. Her mother now lived in Arizona (Arizona?). Her father was still in Cleveland. And her baby brother, now a banker and father of two (!)—could I believe it? (no)—lived in Virginia. There was more on her life, in a beautiful town not far from a lake; her new passion for boating (as I remembered it, she didn't even swim); the friends she had made there. She sounded happy.

She thought it was sensational that I had actually written a book; she wanted to hear all my other news (what other news?); and—here was the real point of the letter—she was coming to New York! She was getting married again, to a wonderful man she knew I'd like, and she and her new husband were splurging on a

trip to France for their honeymoon; they were spending a night in the city on their way. Could we get together, have dinner? Would I let her know?

My friend's letter depressed me a lot. I sensed a self-
assurance in it that I myself didn't feel and that made
me doubt the direction my own life was taking. It also
seemed to me that we'd have little basis upon which to
reestablish our friendship after all this time. My friend,
with all the conventional adult responsibilities I had
avoided for so long and now wanted, sounded so much
more grown-up than I felt. Suddenly my life, which for
all its ups and downs had seemed okay until the letter
came, now seemed barren. My friend had husbands, a
child, house, washing machine, even her boating. She
was starting a new life, wanted a career; maybe she
would be a sea captain. The possibilities for her
seemed endless.

I, on the other hand, lived in an average apartment I
felt I'd outgrown, had a boyfriend (but with whom
nothing was certain) and the beginnings of a writing
career, along with a full-time job I knew I didn't want
forever. I worried all the time about what was going to
happen next, never felt settled, or safe. Like her, I had
friends I cared about. My cat, Ariel, had died a short
time before. Once in a while, I dropped in on an exer-
cise class. My friend's letter almost clattered with the
comings and goings of the people in her life; now, in
contrast, my life seemed too tidy to me, a life in need
of some tracked-in dirt, or the cheerful sounds of
screen doors slamming.

Her letter came at a bad time. My newer friends—
many of them men and women with fast-track careers—and I had only begun to confess to one another

first-time urges we were discovering in ourselves, longings to settle down, start families, even to own washing
machines. We felt not quite whole and yet tired, as if
our career-centered lives were at the same time too
busy and not busy enough. More and more, I was invited to weddings, baby showers, housewarmings. The
restlessness I was feeling would come and go in intensity, but it never entirely went away anymore. So what
if I had a job some people might envy, or a life that
was, even I had to admit it sometimes, pretty exciting?
So what if I had written a book? Now I looked at my
book, sitting on my coffee table, in disgust. You can't
kiss a book good morning, or make love to it at night,
tuck it in and read it a story, or carry its picture around
in your wallet. You can't even wash clothes in it. What
good is a book?

In my envy, all I could hope for was that my friend
would still wear her hair in that ridiculous flip, or that
too much sun from too much boating would have
ruined her looks forever. Maybe, despite the washing
machine, her new husband would have ring around
the collar. On these slim possibilities, I wrote to tell her
how much I'd love to see her.

As it turned out, there was little need to worry; during our visit, my friend and I got along as well as we
always had. Different as we may be now, we ran out of
time long before we ran out of things to talk about. I
had more to report to her than I thought I would, and
she seemed eager to hear about the writers I'd met
through my work, the restaurants and clubs I'd been to,
and the details of my working life ("You have an *expense
account?*"). My career intrigued her most. "I wonder,"
she said, "if I could ever catch up." I assured her she
could and warned her against over-romanticizing my

life: What I had been wondering, I told her, was whether I could ever catch up with *her*.

She seemed skeptical, however; she seemed to think that my self-sufficiency, my relative freedom, should have brought with it a kind of mystical self-discovery. "You must know who you are," she insisted, and I told her I wasn't at all sure I did, or even what that meant. I was surprised to detect a note of wistfulness in her voice, and I was also surprised that, with a new husband, a child, a boat, a washing machine, and a rich, full life to help define her, she still felt, much as I did, that something was missing from her life. From here, our discussion predictably turned to the familiar, quasi-psychological "how do I find out who I am?" rap that, having engaged in it probably a thousand times— as who hasn't?—I can by now conduct comfortably in my sleep.

But as I thought over our conversation later, it struck me that a satisfying career wouldn't "cure" my friend's uneasiness, any more than a family and a Maytag would tell me, once and for all, who I am. You can't solve a metaphysical problem with a vice-presidency, a bouncy two-year-old, or any other life-style props. I've met people who really do seem, in the popular phrase of our day, to have it all—family, career, good health, material comforts, food processor, and the rest of it— and even they continue to search for something else: their identities, their souls, call it what you like. And even they, or maybe especially they, find their true "identities" as elusive as Tinkerbell's shadow.

"Identity formation," writes one of our widely praised contemporary experts on the life cycle, "is a label for the evolution of the self during the ages six-

teen to twenty-two." Right. "While busily preparing
our career," he adds sternly, "we're engaged in evolving a fuller, more independent adult consciousness."
Yes, sir! With that identity we launch ourselves into the
world, which, according to another expert, should take
us from age twenty-two to twenty-eight. Fine. But even
now, at twenty-eight, we're not remotely out of the
woods.

Between the ages of twenty-eight and thirty-two, according to yet another expert following the same
theme, our independent adult consciousness more or
less intact, we become restless to alter our identity or
add to it, to be something more. Great! And by age
thirty-five, we're on to other identity crises, we're like
trains stopping at every station—but going where? On
the road to identity, to adulthood, to enlightenment?
What is identity, anyway? And what about my friend
and me, who ended our reunion afraid that neither of
us had one? Who were we? Developmental orphans?

I have a close friend whom I see at least every few
weeks or so and who, over the past several months, has
been preoccupied with his new wallet, an elaborate
leather one with plenty of slots for I.D. and credit
cards. Until now, he has prided himself on having little
need for such bourgeois accessories as wallets and I.D.s
and credit cards, but this wallet has brought out a curious change in him. When he first bought it, he already
had an I.D. card from the company where he works;
that filled one slot. A membership card from his gym
took up the second, and his check-cashing card the
third. He was determined, he said, to fill up all the rest
of the slots, ten in all.

The next time I saw him, he had applied for and

already received several credit cards, which he showed me; Visa and MasterCard must have wondered how they had let a man in his thirties with a good job slip through their fingers all these years. A New Yorker who had never learned to drive, my friend announced he was now taking driving lessons. Soon a driver's license and a car-rental card would fill the seventh and eighth slots. The ninth was given over to miscellaneous business cards, including that of his recently enlisted stockbroker. A new library card took up the tenth.

Last week he showed me the now filled-up wallet, his name embossed on at least nine different documents; he was delighted with himself. By this time I had figured out what he was up to: "So now do you know who you are?" I asked him. "I know who I am on paper," he said, "and plastic. It says so right here," he added, pointing again to his cards and acting only mildly sheepish. From my own experience, I can add that to lose a wallet, with all your credit and credentials inside, is to feel without identity, to feel that you left yourself on a store counter or in the back of a taxi, or that possibly someone else is up to no good with your credit cards. Without your credentials, you can't prove you exist.

On the first level in the—let's call it—"identity pyramid," my friend with his wallet is right. I have papers; therefore I am. You were born? Birth certificate. You work? Social Security card. Own a car? Title, registration, insurance papers. Own a house? More papers. Married? Marriage license. Divorced? Divorce decree. Still more papers follow you when you die, to prove that you once were alive; no doubt papers are required to get you into heaven. These papers are there for all the world to see, and in the simplest sense, the more papers you have, the more layers there are to your life. In his frantic rush to acquire the papers to fill his new wallet, my friend must have been—he was, actually—in the midst of a real identity crunch.

An identity pyramid built of paper obviously means next to nothing in itself; the reality, alas, is yourself sweating in the gym, and not the card that tells you you belong. It's when the paper identity meets real life, at the second level of the pyramid, that our identities begin to take on substance. Here we are as others see us—as husband, wife, someone's child, lover, friend, colleague, whatever; here we are as we go about our day-to-day lives. To a large extent, as was well said in a recent survey on American life, "We discover who we are face to face and side by side with others in work, love, and learning. All of our activity goes on in relationships, groups, associations, and communities ordered by institutional structures and interpreted by cultural patterns of meaning."

Nevertheless, to take stock of who we are through these external relationships still gets us only partway to a definition of the self: Relationships are fluid, volatile, dependent on outside circumstances, while the "who am I" kind of identity that my childhood friend and I, for all our very real attachments to the world, were groping for is an inner self (or so we imagined) that is fixed, dependable, and strong enough to see you through the failure or disruption of any of these outside relations. You might sustain yourself with your identity as the perfect husband, only to be continually thwarted by a less than perfect wife—or find that to be the wife you'd like to be takes away from being the mother you know you can be, or the professional success you also want to be.

Insofar as our relations are concerned, from what I've seen, we tend not to validate our identities by accepting our flawed selves as they are; instead we see ourselves as what we can become. No one, or at least no one with normal impulses, gives up: We struggle for life, a better life, and more and more of it, from the moment we're born. In other words, my identity lies not in the pointless fight I've just started with my boyfriend, but in knowing that I'll "do better next time." I am not the person who was late turning in an assignment to a respected colleague, I am the person who won't be late with the next one. I am not the person who just gossiped about a friend and hated myself afterward, but the one who will make it up to that friend. I am the person I will be when I'm perfect.

But who am I in the meantime?

It's this third tier of the identity pyramid I find most troublesome, as I try to make the acquaintance of my inner self, or my "self of selves," as William James called it. I'm not sure *identity* is a complete enough word for what I'm looking for; I want not only to know my inner self but also to *like* her. Words like *self-esteem, self-acceptance, self-approval,* and *self-respect* come to mind, and also words like *character, honor, goodness*—not scientific words, to be sure, but the soul can't be measured scientifically. Nor does it turn up automatically when you're twenty-two, twenty-eight, or thirty-five. This admittedly vague need for a fixed identity—a soul, for want of a better word—is what my friend and I were asking each other how to find, and our question, according to a 1961 essay on the familiar problem of alienation as a response to our complex, industrialized, and fast-moving world, "is not simple to answer":

> It has haunted many people increasingly in the last hundred years. They no longer feel certain who they are because in modern industrial society . . . they are alienated from nature, alienated from their fellow men, alienated from the work of their hands and minds, and alienated from themselves.

The more rootless the society, the greater one's need to find an internal constant, to befriend one's self, or even to become one's own best friend, as a 1973 best-seller urged us all to do. Ernest G. Schachtel, a part of whose essay I've just quoted, goes on to argue that such a search for identity is self-defeating. Self-absorption is not the same, Schachtel points out, as self-knowledge.

To raise the "who am I" question obsessively, as millions of Americans began doing in the sixties and still do, is like playing the children's game of "Statues," where you run around until the leader says, "Freeze," and then you stop moving. Usually in the game you end up in an uncomfortable position, or an unattractive one; often you're off in a corner of the game and can't see the other players. However you freeze, all you can think about is keeping the posture. The other statues cease to matter. In the search for self, where could you possibly freeze yourself? At that moment when you were so proud of having done something genuinely, selflessly good? If that's to be your standard, then you'll rarely live up to it. That self will disappoint you constantly. Should you freeze your "self" at the

moment when you made a fool of yourself at a business meeting and everyone laughed? If you do, you'll
never get your confidence back. What's more, if you
freeze at that moment in the meeting, you will lose
sight of the fact that everyone else has forgotten the
remark and gone on with the meeting, and that everyone else makes equally stupid remarks from time to
time. To fixate on the self, in other words, is to allow
the self to take on a grander perspective than it should.
One dumb comment in a meeting is just that—it's what
you did, not who you are. In "Statues," the winner
holds his pose the longest; in life it's the other way
around.

This practice of self-examination can be particularly
damaging nowadays, for the rhetorical imperative of
our own self-help era demands that we continually
scrutinize not only ourselves but our mates, our jobs,
our friends, our lives, even our shrinks, to make certain that they are providing us with optimum happiness. The point instead is that the only way to be
your own best friend is to be someone else's best friend
first. Schachtel, a disciple of William James whether he
knows it or not, calls this "productive self knowledge:
to pay attention to what one is actually doing in his
relation to others, to the world and—we might add—
to himself."

To put it in a harsher way, the more you question
yourself and your identity, the more you'll fall short of
who you want to be and who you think you should be:
the more you'll hate yourself for your own imperfec-
tions and the world's. For example, if in my search for
"identity," I ask myself (as I have), "Am I really the
kind of person who can watch other people starving on

the evening news and then go out to a lavish dinner?"
I'd have to admit that, yes, I've done that. And if that's
me, if that's my *self,* then I'd have to despise who I
am—and in the process help neither the starving nor
myself. If I'm engaged in a conversation and wondering what *I'm* going to say next, I won't hear what the
other person has to say. If I worry that *I* don't know
how to comfort a friend in distress, I'm not able to put
myself in my friend's shoes and offer comfort spon-
taneously. To overanalyze ourselves is, ironically, to assume that we're more important in relation to the rest
of the world than any of us could possibly be. If I keep
on reaching for my identity by looking only inside myself, then after failing to help the starving, my conversation, and my friend, I won't be able to keep from
asking, "How could I possibly like myself, with all my
guilt, shame, faults, and demons?" By then, it's too late
to help; I'd never be able to help enough to ensure my
own self-approval. So without fail, the unavoidable
final question is: "If I'm so terrible, how could anybody
else possibly like me?"

The psychiatrist Carl Jung's essay "The Stages of
Life," first published in book form in 1933, offers the
following sensible warning: *"For a young person it is almost a sin—and certainly a danger—to be too much occupied
with himself; but for the ageing person it is a duty and a
necessity to give serious attention to himself."* Jung's warning
is particularly apt for my contemporaries and me: if
the external benchmarks of adulthood are lacking (or
slow in coming), surely the internal benchmarks will be
just as elusive.

Jung is not saying that the young person, whom he

defines as under forty, give or take, should never be reflective; his carefully worded phrase advises that it's dangerous for him to be "too much" occupied with himself early on. He argues convincingly that the first half of an adult life well-lived must be devoted to "our entrenchment in the outer world," and the second half, to our entrenchment in our inner worlds. I suspect Jung would have had little patience with the conversation between my friend and me, when we were idly wondering "who we were," and whining about identity crises and so on. He would have known that the "identity" we were looking for is not something you're born with and can find readily by looking for it, like perfect pitch or a talent for painting, but something that you work to build in relation to others. We find our identities not in contemplation but in action. What would be the point, Jung might have asked my friend and me, of probing your inner nature now, while it's still developing? How can you hope to read the book of your life before you've written it?

Writing at about the same time as Jung, but from a wholly different perspective, the philosopher Bertrand Russell, attempting to define happiness, talked about his deeply unhappy childhood; he remembered figuring out, at the age of five, that if he were to live to be seventy, he would now have lived only one-fourteenth of his entire life. At five, "I felt the long-spread-out boredom ahead of me to be almost unendurable." In fact Russell lived to be ninety-eight and published the third and last volume of his autobiography at age ninety-seven, in 1969. Much earlier, though, in 1930, thinking back to himself at age five, he wrote: "Now, on the contrary, I enjoy life; I might almost say that with every year that passes I enjoy it more. . . . Very largely [this] is due to a diminishing preoccupation with myself." Had Russell heard the conversation between my friend and me, he might have said, "Of course you don't know who you are. You're looking *inside* to find out, when you should be looking *outside*." Of his own road to happiness, he wrote: "Gradually I learned to be indifferent to myself and my deficiencies; I came to center my attention increasingly upon external objects: the state of the world, various branches of knowledge, individuals for whom I felt affection."

Identity, in other words, is something like Louis Armstrong's famous definition of jazz: If you have to ask, you'll never know. Better just to let it happen.

| 8 |

ALONE

He went into the kitchen and took a roll of liverwurst from the yellowed refrigerator. Leaning against the sink, paring off slices with a rusty knife, he ate liverwurst until he stopped feeling hungry and then put it away again. That was his supper. There was a table, of course, and two chairs, and a whole set of dishes in the cupboard (his mother's gift, brown earthenware), but he rarely used them. Most meals he ate standing at the stove, spooning large mouthfuls directly from the pot to save dishwashing. . . .

Then sometimes, when living alone depressed him, he set the table meticulously with knife, fork and spoon and a folded napkin, plate and salad plate, salt and pepper shakers. He served into serving dishes, and from them to his plate, as if he were two people performing two separate tasks. He settled himself in his chair and smoothed the napkin across his knees; then he sat motionless . . . stunned by the dismalness of this elaborate table set for one. What was he doing here, twenty-eight years old and all alone? Why was he living like an elderly widower in this house without children, set in his ways, pottering from stove to table to sink?

—ANNE TYLER, *The Clock Winder*

Some years ago, when I was coming out of a particularly bleak phase of my life and moving into what I hoped would be a happier one, I was invited by someone I hardly knew to a New Year's Eve party, at a stranger's SoHo loft. It was to begin that evening at eleven and last till "whenever." "Amazing loft," said my benefactor, who offered more details about the party: There would be "hundreds" of people there, he said, and he thought I would probably know lots of them, which I myself doubted; and the loft, he promised, had an "impressive sound system," which I knew meant that the music would be loud. There would be free champagne and old movies in a special room.

Another of the evening's highlights was to be helium, which at that time was a favored, and as far as I know, a perfectly legal party diversion. Waist-high tanks of it are used to fill up balloons, and when you breathe in the helium from the balloon and try to talk, you sound like Donald Duck. I had done helium in this way a few times at other parties and knew that helium does make for a very funny party, indeed. "Oh, helium," I found myself saying. "Terrific."

I tried to imagine going to that party—dressed up, alone, making my way downtown and then back home in the sometimes sinister carnival atmosphere that is New Year's Eve in New York. I wished I were the kind of person who could simply go to such a party, trust that I'd meet someone interesting, and have a good time in the bargain. That social, however, I am not.

Instead, though I was cheered by the invitation, all I could think was: Why go to all that trouble to spend an evening talking—assuming I could find somebody to talk to—like Donald Duck? And so, once it became clear that no other invitations would be forthcoming, I decided to celebrate New Year's Eve at home by myself.

To my surprise, I began to plan my "party" with great care. I spent two days preparing. First I cleaned my apartment until the whole thing (both rooms, that is) smelled of wax and polish. I bought flowers, candles, bubble bath, and a satiny new bathrobe on sale. I went to a bookstore and bought Barbara Pym's latest novel, read the first chapter, then made myself put it down until the "party." I also bought three new record albums (Chopin, Keith Jarrett, and Bob Marley), justifying the expense by estimating what New Year's Eve out, with taxis and so on, would cost. My menu was easy—pâté, cheeses, French bread, apples, wine, fresh espresso beans mixed with cinnamon for coffee, and a few tiny cookies from a nearby bakery that even from the outside smells like butter. It was almost dark when I finished my shopping, and the streets were beginning to clear, as everyone rushed home, I supposed, to dress for lavish auld lang syne dinners and parties with spouses, lovers, intimate friends.

I had expected to feel at least a little bit lonely that night, but I didn't; I wasn't even aware, so absorbed was I in my novel and music, and tucked up in a blanket, when midnight approached and passed. This, I remember thinking, was living alone at its best, choosing my own life, treating myself as I would a welcome guest. At other times I would think of my apartment almost as a hotel room, somewhere to change clothes and sleep, a place to be during the pauses in my life. That night, however, it felt like a real home. It was about two in the morning when I finally finished my book, turned off the stereo, and fell into an easy sleep in my freshly made bed. I felt proud of my experiment in happy solitude in a way I couldn't explain.

I felt at peace again the next morning, and at a New Year's Day lunch with a few friends. Yet right after lunch, I found myself eager to go home again, back to the contentment I'd known the night before. And that made me nervous. I wondered: Am I becoming too adept at living alone, at being alone? Am I becoming too comfortable in my unnaturally monastic life? I wasn't always alone, of course, and when I was alone I wasn't always happy that way. But now it scared me to think that perhaps the safe little life I was building for myself just might become my only life after all. And it scared me even more to think that this solitary life of mine might one day come to seem like enough.

In 1980, according to the Census report, 27 percent of all American household units—or 18 million of us— were made up of people living alone. This is a higher percentage than ever before and shows every sign that it will continue to grow. At present, more women (of whom 40 million are single but not necessarily by themselves) than men live alone, but there are more women than men to begin with, and the number of men living alone has also been rising sharply over the past fifteen years. Eight million of us living alone are sixty-five or older. Still, as the age at which we marry inches up and the frequency with which we marry inches down, to say nothing of our 50-percent divorce rate, the statistical likelihood that each of us will spend at least a part of our adult lives alone increases. I don't think it's stretching the point to suggest that living alone—or at least facing the possibility that we might eventually have to, or want to, live alone—with the day-to-day self-reliance this arrangement demands, is almost a criterion of adulthood in our time.

Whereas a generation ago, as we've seen, family togetherness was the desperate if unnatural catchword, today our popular wisdom dictates that the stronger we are as individuals the more satisfactory our relationships will be. A major study on contemporary American life reports: "To summarize the changes in the American family since the early nineteenth century, the network of kinship has narrowed and the sphere of individual decision has grown." Strengthening and defending this "sphere of individual decision" has become more important than ever before, as our extended ties not only to family but also to our communities have weakened. Living alone is, of course, the ultimate test of our capacity to thrive within this sphere of individual decision.

There's a recent television commercial—an ad for telephones—which shows a young man in a big, sparsely furnished room, talking to his father on the phone and saying something like, "Living alone is fabulous, Dad. So many friends, parties . . . And," he continues bravely, "the privacy is great." By the end of the commercial, it's agreed that Dad will come over to watch the game on TV, bring a pizza, and in effect save his son from a slide into loneliness and possibly starvation. The telephone, of course, has been the son's lifeline. The commercial should be poignant, but instead it's funny, for the viewer believes that the young man is facing a familiar rite of passage and will pass the test: He *will* make friends and go to parties, he'll come to cherish his privacy, and one day, perhaps when he's married and the father of six, he'll look back fondly to this simpler stage of his life. And often that's more or less how it works.

My friends in New York are outspoken on the pros and cons of living alone (except for a county in Hawaii comprised of a leper colony, Manhattan is the only county in the United States with an average household size of fewer than two people); most people I know, New Yorkers or not, have lived alone at one time or another or do so now. Their consensus—even among those who choose or prefer to live alone—is this: "I'm happy to have done it, to have survived it." Veterans often speak of living alone as a test of will and inner strength, not unlike making it through the Outward Bound wilderness-survival program: If I know I can live alone, I don't have to be afraid of it. If I can make it on my own, I will never have to depend entirely on anyone else to keep me alive. The ability to live alone is like having a stash of emotional security hidden under the mattress.

Developmental psychology has little to say on the single life and how it fits into the life cycle; in the early postwar years, as we've seen, spinsterhood, bachelorhood, divorce, and especially homosexuality were thought to be frivolous and selfish or, at any rate, aberrant ways of life. Developmentally speaking, single people simply have not counted. One expert, who allows that it's normal enough today to be single for a few years before you marry, also promises that living

alone in middle age can be, at least for a woman, a
relief from the drudgery of taking care of the husband
and children the author assumes she has somehow
managed to escape. Another book covers the single life
in fewer than ten lines: "As a single we have freedom
to move about, but we have little opportunity to move
in, to probe ourself [*sic*] and others deeply. Our childhood habits, protective devices and demons are not
challenged with the same intensity found in couples living together." I would disagree. I have found that living alone provides if anything too much opportunity to
probe oneself, and that when you're up against your
childish habits and demons alone, you will call upon
inner resources you'd never discover with someone else
to hide behind.

When I was first on my own in New York, I lived
with roommates and then, when I was twenty-four and
mistakenly thought I was as grown-up as I'd ever be, I
lived for a time with a man. Afterward I lived alone for
the first time, in a good-sized studio apartment, by
Manhattan standards, that I felt lucky to find. I had
often longed for a privacy so complete. I felt ready for
it and looked forward to my new freedom and the
chance to find out what I was like to live with.

I was not great to live with.

After the initial settling in—should I put my fork
here, or here?—I saw for the first time just how much
I had always depended upon the others I'd always had
around me for company, approval, and social lead-
ership. Back then, I was shy about suggesting social
plans to people I didn't know well and shyer still about
entertaining on my own. I discovered with dismay that
one day I'd be compulsively neat (once I cleaned the

baseboards of my studio with a toothbrush) and the next day so sloppy I shocked even myself. Some weekends I would be as reclusive as Howard Hughes, pretending not to be home or to be busy if someone called; other times I would go out even when I didn't want to, just to have company other than myself. I ate only packaged foods, the more chemicals listed on the package the better. I was not proud of the way I was coping.

At first I wondered if I were the kind of person who could function only when someone else would soon be home to "watch" me function; I felt strangely self-conscious on my own, as if I could perform the routine acts of graceful living only on someone else's behalf. I would never, for example, have served the man I'd lived with granola for supper, straight from the box, as I served myself now; I'd at least have served it in a bowl, maybe added a salad. I had to learn the lesson that I've since watched others, old and young, single and divorced, struggling to understand: When you live alone, you have to become both the giver and the recipient in your own life. There was a larger lesson I was learning, too, though I didn't know it till much later, when I was living with another man and very much in love. It had nothing to do with soup for one or adjusting to living in a single room; it was a lesson I'd have had to master even if I'd lived as a princess in a grand palace or as the benevolent matriarch in a boisterous household of my own. What I was also beginning to understand is that we all of us, regardless of our circumstances, live alone.

It wasn't long before I stopped tiptoeing around my studio and began to fill it up, the way an actor takes over a stage. I developed my own rituals and rhythms, just as I had in any other living arrangement I'd known, and living alone came to seem, not natural, exactly, but no longer, well, weird. As other people I know have confirmed, you have to work at living alone, just as you have to work at a relationship or a marriage. It takes practice.

"You have to feel civilized when you live alone," says a man I know, who until recently had lived alone for many years. "You know, have routines: Hang up your clothes, even if nobody else is there to see you." You'll come to take pleasure in the small rituals that make up your life: "Fresh orange juice every day," says another male friend. "I squeeze it myself. It's an indulgence—oranges are expensive—but it seems like something real to do." "Sunday nights I always stay home, always order Chinese food, and do all the things I have to do, laundry, pay bills, before Monday," a woman I used to work with says. "I love being orderly in my own way." I began to develop habits of my own, too, to buy fresh flowers with every paycheck, to grind my coffee the night before, to shape my domestic arrangements in the way I'd hoped I would. I was pleased with my privacy, my independence. I began to learn about living alone, and also about being alone—different matters entirely.

"I had a roommate before I lived alone," one friend says, "and one adjustment when she moved out was that I was used to things happening all by themselves. If there's someone else around, you only have to work half as hard at your life. If she got invited to a party, I'd just go, too. Or if on a Saturday night we were both free, we could go to the movies or stay home, make popcorn, and watch TV, or someone else could come over. You don't realize how social you are automatically just by having someone else there. When you're alone, not much will happen unless you make it happen." What my friend saw, to put it another way, was the risk, in living alone, of fading into your own solitude.

"I know what that's like," says a friend who has lived alone ("this time") for eight or nine years. "It's different during the week; you run around more. There are always things to do after work. But on the weekends, if I don't make plans, sometimes I spend too much time alone. Maybe it's just me, but if you don't make an effort you can begin to feel pretty cut off. By Sunday, you don't even want to see anybody, you're so out of touch." This feeling, which I've known, too, isn't loneliness but isolation.

In an essay on the difference between isolation and loneliness in contemporary life, Peter Townsend clarifies the distinction: "To be socially isolated is to have few contacts with family and community; to be lonely is to have an unwelcome *feeling* of lack or loss of companionship." In other words, to be isolated means that you're simply not in touch with the world around you, that, for whatever reason, you've cut yourself off, or perhaps you never managed to be connected to it in the first place. The possibilities for connectedness are endless, and not simply social; as E. M. Forster wrote, "Only connect." A scientist in her lab, a painter in his studio, a poet—all are alone but not isolated. A man writing a love letter is not isolated, nor is someone walking along a beach, playing catch with a puppy, making a happy-birthday call, playing a piano, or planting bulbs in the fall to come up in the spring. I know married people who seem to me to be painfully isolated and people who live alone whose connections to the world are many and real. I was alone that New Year's Eve, but I had my book and my music; had I gone to the party, I don't doubt that I would have been unbearably isolated, and lonely besides. For loneliness is something different—something that everyone feels, at times. Loneliness is what we feel when we really know that, for all our connections, we're finally alone.

"We are born helpless," wrote C. S. Lewis in his book *The Four Loves*. "As soon as we are fully conscious we discover loneliness. . . . Our whole being by its very nature is one vast need; incomplete, preparatory, empty yet cluttered, crying out for Him who can untie things that are now knotted together and tie up things that are still dangling loose." Loneliness, in other words, comes with the human territory. Lewis is saying that nothing—not marriage, not friendship, not the perfect spin on a tennis serve, or money or even God—can finally protect us against loneliness. And what my friend realized when he said, "If you don't make an effort, you can begin to feel pretty cut off," is that you can, you must, fight isolation, no matter what your living arrangements happen to be. To fight isolation, a sensation perhaps more piercing when you live alone, is to face adult life. Loneliness, on the other hand, is something we all have to learn to accept.

I used to patronize a small neighborhood bank, a branch office of a larger bank. It was convenient, but more than that, I liked the few people who worked there; this big-city bank had an old-fashioned, small-town feeling. There was one particularly friendly teller who came to call me by name—and my name has never been one to make bank tellers jump to attention. I'd go to the bank at least every two weeks to deposit my paycheck, and often this teller and I would chat for a minute or two. Once, when I was there to deposit my check as usual, she stamped the deposit slip and then looked up at me with a smile of pleasure: "You got a raise," she said. "Congratulations." Then she seemed to catch herself—the bank had probably told her to pretend not to notice her depositors' shifting fortunes. But I thought her comment was charming; I liked it that she seemed happy for me.

Now I use another bank, and mostly I withdraw and deposit money into a machine with my cash card and a secret code number, a tamper-proof jumble of the numbers in my birthdate. But I thought of that teller the other day, after my bank machine and I had a fight over whether it would give me back my card, after making several calls and leaving as many messages at as many beeps, after staring for hours at my word-processing screen—after a perfectly ordinary postindustrial day. I wasn't lonelier or any more alienated than usual that day. Instead, I was having an attack of the kind of aloneness Emerson in his essay on self-reliance called "mechanical" isolation.

To read "Self-Reliance" is, or is for me anyway, to feel inadequate; Emerson demands more from the self than I know how to give. He writes: "I shun father and mother and wife and brother when my genius calls me." I'm more the type who is easily diverted from her work when anyone even mentions going to the movies. "If we live truly, we shall see truly," he writes. I'm not always strong enough for that. "It is easy," he writes, "in the world to live after the world's opinion; it is easy in solitude to live after our own; but the great man is he who in the midst of the crowd keeps with perfect sweetness the independence of solitude." What Emerson is saying is that our primary obligation is to our selves, to make our own lives, to express our New World freedom, and to understand that everything else—love, charity, a meaningful life—comes only out of that perfect, private loyalty to the self.

He saw the enemies of self-reliance in the social roles we take on, the compromises we make in our jobs, our easy concessions to the manners and fashions of our times, "the forced smile which we put on in company where we do not feel at ease, in answer to conversation which does not interest us." Each such encounter empties the soul, and the soul, Emerson felt, is not readily replenished.

What he also saw early on, with stunning foresight, was that as machines increasingly take over the functions of a human group, the more detached the members of the group will become. Imagine a group of people holding hands in a circle. Now imagine the same group, twice as large, but each person is holding hands with a machine on either side: The machines link the group and at the same time separate it. "The civilized man has built a coach, but has lost the use of his feet," Emerson writes. "He has got a fine Geneva watch, but he has lost the skill to tell the hour by the sun." He has a high-tech bank card, but he misses his bank teller.

I have a friend who almost always prefers going to the movies alone, so that she can concentrate on the film without the distraction of a companion; she's forgotten the pleasure of comparing impressions after the credits. I've seen families who watch TV during dinner, and husbands and wives who claim to be happy and yet pride themselves on their "absolutely separate lives." I know people, married and single, so afraid to be alone (or together) that they're out night after night, or if they're not, they're drowning out the sounds of their selves with the electronic music of the stereo or the canned laughter of the TV. I myself know how easy—easier than in Emerson's day—it is to slip into mechanical oblivion, to get used, for example, to long phone chats, where you can't see your friends' expressions, instead of visits, or to use a tanning machine (this at least I haven't done) instead of seeking out the sun.

"We must go alone," Emerson writes. "I like the silent church before the service begins, better than any preaching. . . . But your isolation must not be mechanical, but spiritual, that is, must be elevation." He's saying that it is essential for us to be able to experience privately the serenity of the quiet sanctuary. But he's also reminding us that it is not okay to have no one to go to church with, metaphorically speaking, to share a hymnal with once the service begins—or to go to lunch with afterward. He's saying that meaningful self-reliance is self-reliance you share.

| 9 |

KINSHIP

Late last spring, I spent a long, memorable evening with a woman I didn't know well—I'll call her Elizabeth. Our meeting wasn't planned; we just happened to find ourselves together, staying with mutual friends at their beach house in East Hampton. Our friends had invited us to a party that night, but we both declined, preferring to stay home and "play country," as Elizabeth put it. We ended up taking a long walk on the beach, and then, in borrowed sweaters and over too many cups of coffee, talked on the terrace until our friends arrived home after midnight.

Such unexpected occasions are cozy to begin with, and by the end of the evening, after an experimental exchange of certain confidences, we were on our way to a possible friendship. The conversation that night covered familiar ground (our work, the state of the world, the horrible things men can do), but mostly

what we ended up talking about was similar and painful experiences we'd had when close friendships, not
romances, we'd known had come to an end.

After college and a year or two of "hanging out"
during the sixties, Elizabeth had come to New York
some twenty years earlier with the vague urge to be a
graphics designer and with design credentials that
were even more vague. When she arrived at Penn Station, well after midnight, she went to stay with an old
schoolmate and the next day called a woman whose
number someone had given her—a friend of a friend,
"someone in design." The woman had agreed to see
her, maybe help her get started, but this "someone in
design," as it turned out, was not actually *in* design but
worked in a downtown warehouse at the bottom rung
of the "stepladder" of a struggling design firm whose
star was a volatile man in his early thirties. One thing
led to another, and Elizabeth and her new mentor,
who with her greater experience soon began to think
that two designers might be better than one, became
close friends and began to chart their futures. Elizabeth also befriended her mentor's roommate, an aspiring restauranteur. Before long, as she remembers it,
the three women were inseparable. "You wouldn't believe how close we were," she told me. "One of us
would get a cat and the cat would belong to all of us.
Nobody would have a boyfriend who couldn't accept
the whole package."

Eventually the two designers opened their own small
firm, and the restauranteur became one of several
partners in a trendy restaurant (decorated by her
friends' design firm: "The restaurant looks like an ad
for a restaurant"); all three were concerned about

keeping their successes pretty much equal and were careful not to disrupt the balance of the friendship. Among the three, there were two marriages over the years, and two divorces, one remarriage, a couple of live-in arrangements, two kids, assorted pets, shared cars, and myriad boyfriends. At times, the three lived together, notably "in the summers, when we'd always rent a house—the same house, full of sand—at the Jersey shore. We did that for about eight years. I was married for part of that time, and I think my husband sometimes felt like he was the guest and we were the family. But we all had fun—all sorts of company, and we got to know tons of people together. And there were the kids by then, so it did seem like a real family. We all helped." But over the past couple of years this makeshift family has begun to self-destruct, in ways that are hard to put a finger on.

For one thing, one of the women has now remarried, and she and her husband have bought a house "on their own," and not even at the Jersey shore. The design firm "is having 'underground' fights over certain accounts and about whether we should spend more money on fancier offices. We don't really talk about it, but there's this tension." The restauranteur is thinking of opening a second restaurant in another city. The three women, now in their early to middle forties, are, in various degrees, feeling the pull to go their separate ways—and all are suffering from it. "Sometimes when we're all together now, it's fine; it's the way it's always been," Elizabeth says. "But most of the time, we look at one another and we all know it's over. No one will admit it, but it's not the same anymore. This for me is worse than my divorce was."

I knew how she felt: A little "family" of mine, a close friendship that had meant a lot to me for a number of years, was breaking up for good at about that time, too, and I was surprised at how painful such a loss could be. Like Elizabeth, I found it hard to talk about the collapse of a relationship that until recently had been one of the sturdiest pillars of my life.

Against all likely New York odds, I'd met my friend when she moved into the building where I'd had my first studio apartment. She was a few years older than I and rented what seemed to me a palatial one-bedroom apartment not too long after I'd moved in. A string of coincidences—she was also in publishing, worked not far from my office, and left for work about the same time I did—brought us together, and soon we were beyond the pleasant-smile stage that New Yorkers think of as neighborliness. Off and on, we'd meet to walk home from work together and end up having dinner on the way; we joined a health club in the neighborhood. After several guarded months we were as good as roommates, but better, I thought, because we had the privacy of our own apartments. I loved knowing that a friend lived nearby. One common fear among people living alone is that if you slip or lose your balance, you inevitably worry, "Oh, now I'll fall and be killed, and no one will ever find me." I recall thinking that, with my friend right upstairs, now at least I'd be found if I slipped and died. Not to be morbid about it, I knew I'd also "find" her too if something happened. The thought was oddly comforting.

Throughout the years of our friendship, there grew a real sense that we were in some ways responsible for each other. She had family, and so did I, but there we were anyway, in closer day-to-day touch with each other than with our families and other friends. Walking home from work, we would air the day's grievances, so that the devious workings of office politics wouldn't haunt us late at night and when we were alone. Like air-traffic controllers, we each tracked the other's life—"So how did that lunch go today?" During lonely times, we forced ourselves to get out and do something; we met each other's various friends. In general, we checked in every day or two, even if there was nothing new to report.

The rupture must have started long before it came out into the open, and I was never clear about the sequence of our falling out. We both moved, both changed jobs so that our careers were farther apart, both fell in love; the distance between us kept growing. And we both hurt each other unintentionally, I suppose, simply by growing up. Despite the growing hurt, our friendship limped along for a while and now, for all practical purposes, we've abandoned it and gone on to other people and interests. The possibility has lately occurred to me that this friendship, which reminds me so much of a time, a place, and of the matching circumstances that defined our lives back then, was a momentary bubble of safety that inevitably had to burst when we didn't need it anymore. To have kept it going might have meant going backward in our lives, or hanging onto a time we'd both outgrown.

Still, what makes me sad about the breakup, even today, is a memory of the two of us out shopping on a dull, rainy Saturday afternoon, passing the time by trying on ridiculously elaborate hats with veils that we never would have bought, and then a salesclerk asking us if we were sisters. I had wanted to say we were.

In its earliest usage, the word *family* was not limited only to dad, mom, kids, and in the larger sense, grandparents, cousins, and the like. Until the seventeenth century, a family was a household: "In addition to the immediate family," Witold Rybczynski writes in *Home*, the family "included employees, servants, apprentices, friends, and protégés—households of up to twenty-five persons were not uncommon." Nor was the household itself centered around what we think of today as family. According to Peter Laslett in *The World We Have Lost*, and as we've seen, children as young as seven were commonly sent away to learn a trade, other children were brought in as apprentices, and few in-laws or children, once they married, would join the household. Instead, they'd join other family establishments and make household connections of their own. Even in the last century, Joseph Ketts writes in his book on adolescence in America, there were no sacred bonds to hold the family together. Young girls of fifteen would leave home to find jobs in towns as teachers, shopgirls, or factory workers; their brothers, who were more useful on the farm, would leave home a few years later. After such migrations, the children would rarely see their parents but would instead set up kinship networks with neighbors or relatives from home who had already migrated and new coworkers and friends they'd meet in passing—much the way we do now. In other words, to mourn the demise of the family as the predominant social unit in modern Western culture is to mourn a myth.

This is not to belittle family ties—the bonds of blood, history, obligation, property, and sometimes love; those ties are awesome and universal. My family is my family, no matter what. On the other hand, kinship ties, as we'll talk about them here, are instead the friends, acquaintances, and groups that begin making up our lives outside the family from the time our first-grade teachers give us marks for "Social Skills," or when we're chosen (or not) as a teammate on the neighborhood touch football team. According to Robert Ardrey in *The Social Contract,* such groups fill our essential needs of "identity, stimulation, and security." The group instinct, he writes, is inbred:

> The loneliness of a man is the loneliness of the animal. We must have each other. The baboon seeks his troop, the bookkeeper his business office, the buffalo his herd on some far savanna, the weary bricklayer his fellows at the corner pub, the starling his chattering flock among London streets, the hyena his clan, the farmer his wife when the last chores are done, the herring his school in the cold North Sea, all for quite the same reason: because we cannot survive without each other.

Your own kinship groups might include, for example, your smaller corporate "family" within the larger corporation; a group of "Big Chill" friends you see from time to time and who connect you to your past; the social group with whom you and your wife or boyfriend—or just you—feel most relaxed; the members of your poker game, baseball team, or once-a-month lunch club; the people in group therapy with you; your ex-wife or ex-husband; or the deeper friendships in which you'd describe your friend as like a "sister" or "brother." Easy acceptance characterizes such kinship ties, as well as a sense of belonging, though not necessarily intimacy. Ties like these are not always to our closest friends; true friendship is a rare and mystical attachment. Shifting kinship networks that change, grow, and recede in importance throughout our lives tell us who we are and where we've been. If families— or at least blood relations—are fixed, our kinship networks are fluid; they are the living scrapbooks of our lives. "Most anthropologists today," Lillian B. Rubin writes in *Just Friends,* "argue that kinship is as much an *idea*—a system of belief—as it is a biological fact, and that the biological and social relationships need not necessarily coincide."

Thus the figurative extended family can reach beyond legal ties to include attachments from the past (an ex-lover you see once or twice a year, "just to keep up"), present friendships of varying intensities, the members of a household, and people who can comfortably rely upon one another—the way Elizabeth and her friends, or my friend and I, once could—because they want to, and not because ties of guilt or familial obligation force them to. Such surrogate families of circumstance or of one's own choosing can stand in for or enrich the biological family, or, more often, operate as a legitimate kinship unit quite apart from the family itself. Especially today, when a proper legal family is as often as not comprised of changing partners, "steps," "exes," and total strangers—who may be scattered throughout the country, at that—it is consoling to acknowledge and celebrate the family in the largest, most expansive sense possible. If you can measure family ties by love, then a group of old friends sharing their annual Thanksgiving dinner can be as much a family as the posed-for-a-picture Norman Rockwell variety.

In 1980, 60 percent of the households in America were made up of married couples. (A "household" as defined by the Census Bureau can contain roommates, people living alone, or family members—a single parent with children, for example, or two brothers living together, or unmarried partners. Households do not include dorms, prisons, barracks, or other institutional arrangements.) Of these households, half—30 percent of the U.S. total—had children under eighteen living at home and half did not. Slightly over a quarter of American families with children, and 60 percent of black families, are headed by a single parent. One-fifth of white children and almost three-quarters of black children are born to single mothers. As we've seen, slightly more than a quarter of all households are made up of people who live alone. Thus, when we think of the nuclear family as the norm by which to judge our lives, we are measuring ourselves not against a universal standard but against the approximately one-third of the families with children who live together but who no longer represent the cultural norm they seemed to typify in the fifties and sixties.

Our need for alternative supportive ties to the world speaks for itself. As a result, researchers are now re-positioning their views on the importance of the role of friends and social networks in adult development. Rubin reports that, "friends are central actors in the continuing developmental drama of our adulthood . . . . Most modern theorists now understand the formation of a personal identity as a lifetime process to which our varied experiences in the larger social world, as well as in the family, make their contributions. . . . In this process, friends count."

Among the Iroquois, there is no single word meaning "mother" or "father," but only words referring to any male or female kinsperson. The Iroquois family embraces the entire tribe. In Germany, there's a ceremony called the *Duzen*, which publicly formalizes the deepening of a friendship, exalting the bond to one approaching a blood tie. Children in our own culture practice the "blood brother" ritual, and many clubs and organizations refer to members as "sisters," "brother," or just family. The longing to connect, to belong, to give and seek help and care, and to know ourselves through the eyes of others, is powerful; we all want to be part of a family, or many families. No one likes walking into a party—or through life—not knowing a soul.

The other night some friends invited me over for a drink, and once I was there, they decided, as they often do, that I might as well stay for dinner, which was to be a wing-it sort of affair. Their son materialized in time to set the table and, as he was gathering napkins, placemats, and so on, asked if anybody was coming to dinner, so he'd know how many places to set. "No, nobody's coming," his father said, as if to imply: Just family. I pretended to be indignant to be called "nobody," but knew, of course, that I was really being complimented. I therefore figured it was okay to make a show of complaining about the brussels sprouts.

A few summers ago, eight people I know slightly, who themselves weren't all close friends but friendly

acquaintances, rented a house together on Long Island
near the beach and, because I was staying nearby, I was
able to watch them evolve into a family. After the first
weekend, they had managed to turn an impersonal
rental house into a household of their own: They con-
verged upon the house with posters, a stereo, books for
summer reading, a croquet set, pots of geraniums, and
a community canary. One man, whom they called
"General Ted," became the self-appointed cleanup
commander. They shopped, cooked, bickered, teamed
up sometimes like siblings—two against one, or three
against two—and developed a fierce group loyalty that
united them against critical outsiders. *They* were free to
complain about one another, but those of us who
weren't members of the household were not. Over the
course of the summer, one man announced his homosexuality, a secret he still keeps from his parents, to his
summer family and they welcomed his lover into the
fold. The family also supported one woman through
the summer in her efforts to break away from a married man. A dieter in the group was denied ice cream,
a woman who preferred to read all the time was forced
to join in bike trips, and no one who didn't want to be
was ever left alone on a Saturday night. People in families watch out for one another.

This particular group didn't reconvene the following
summer, but the kinship ties remained strong; most of
them are still in touch with the others, even if the family itself meets, like most families, only once in a while.

When other friends of mine, a married couple, re-
built an old Victorian house in the suburbs of Washington and moved there after the birth of their second
child, they chose the paint and wallpaper for their bed-

room and the bedrooms for the kids. "Jeff's room" was another matter. Jeff is their oldest friend, a single man and political consultant whose work takes him all over the world; the closest place he has to a home base is "Jeff's room." "We had ideas for that room," my friends told me. "We wanted to turn it into a library/guest room. But then Jeff showed up with all his bizarre stuff—carved chairs, a temple door—from storage, and a can of red paint. He wanted his room to be red. What do you do?" Nothing. Jeff is family.

Then there's my friend David's "supper club." David works at home and loves to cook. He has lived on his block in Brooklyn, a lovely street lined with turn-of-the-century brownstones, for years, has watched for apartment vacancies, and helped to arrange for a number of his friends to find apartments on the same pretty block. Most of them are single people like himself. Several nights a week, he cooks dinner for whichever of his friends happen to be around, and they in turn chip in for the food. "It'd be sad for us all to be home alone, eating chicken pies night after night," he says. "This works out fine. We don't care if we're boring sometimes, and I can send them home right after dinner if I want to. This isn't entertaining. They're family."

For all the talk about our lonely, isolated society, what I see instead is that we're sorting ourselves into groups, households, friendships, and kinship networks that connect us to our world as surely as the seventeenth-century household with its twenty-five unrelated members was connected to its own world. More and more, I read in the papers about new housing trends, where groups of single people, single parents, or the elderly are adapting single-family neighborhoods into arrangements that are more suitable for the way we live now, or for different American dream "constituencies," as one housing expert calls us all. Three-quarters of all housing in America has been built since 1940, and the housing industry, which, maddeningly, has continued to build larger single-family houses as the average American household size has continued to drop, is finally beginning to reflect America's real housing needs, little by little. There should be room in our world for my friends' summer family, for Jeff, for a single mother I know who has had trouble finding an apartment that permitted children, and for an older married couple who "at this stage" would prefer to live away from the sounds of kids. The point is that we're all "starting" families, all our lives.

Recently, I read an article in *The Wall Street Journal* about older men and women who can't afford to, are afraid to, or don't want to keep up their houses alone anymore. Instead, they're beginning to "experiment with variations on traditional living arrangements. Some are doubling or tripling up with other seniors or with younger housemates. Others are clustering into what their grandchildren a few years back would have called communes." They call themselves "family associations." I was reminded of "Sunnydale Farm," a place a friend and I invented for our old age. "It won't be like this at Sunnydale" is what we're always promising each other. We've invited others in on the joke, and gradually Sunnydale has come to seem real; I can see it in my mind. And maybe we'll actually live there one day.

| 10 |

MEN, WOMEN, EQUALITY, AND LOVE

Not long ago I made plans to meet a married friend at her apartment after work, an hour or so before she expected her husband home for dinner from the racquetball game he played every Tuesday night. That way, we decided, we'd be able to talk by ourselves before her husband and the man I was living with, who had a late meeting, joined us for dinner.

I arrived at the apartment only a moment after Diane did, when she was still taking off her coat and dumping the day's accumulation—briefcase, pocketbook, umbrella, an over-full bag of groceries, a lemon tart in a bakery box, and a lone shoe with a new heel on it—onto the floor. Diane was her customary cheerful and frantic self, and I suddenly felt the adrenaline charge I always get in her company; she's a real-life version of one of those superwomen you read about in magazines, always with energy to spare. A partner in a

large public-relations firm, she has handled her career
as deftly as I've seen other women steer baby strollers
over a curb, and she has always seemed to know exactly
what she wanted: a happy marriage, a high-powered
career, no children, good friends. She also tutors reading one night a week, sews, exercises during her lunch
hour . . . and after I've seen her, I usually go home
and clean out a drawer.

"Pour us a glass of wine while I go change," she ordered, and before I'd even finished with the corkscrew,
Diane had disappeared and reemerged, not an ex-
ecutive in her mid-thirties now, but dressed in cor-
duroys and oversized red sweater, her brown hair in a
ponytail. As we talked, she bustled around, tidying up,
and I followed her from room to room. First she made
the bed, then laid out fresh towels, rinsed the breakfast
coffee from the coffeemaker, threw away the morning
paper, and arranged a bouquet of flowers that had
been sticking out of her briefcase when she got home.
Absently, I found myself helping; I put the umbrella in
its stand, straightened a cushion, wiped off a sticky
countertop. The ritual was familiar: I'd seen women
smoothing out the edges of domestic life for as long as
I can remember, and I've done it myself, willingly or
sometimes resentfully, for a man due home.

While she chopped shallots, I set the table. I told her
about a mutual acquaintance who had lost his job, and
about another, whose good news was that she was
pregnant—she'd wanted a baby for ages. Diane was
worried about someone else we both knew, with boyfriend troubles, who needed to get out more; couldn't
I take her to lunch? She told me about a new account
she had at work, and that she wasn't getting along with

one of her colleagues. Then I tested a theory I was trying to work through for this book, something about the changing roles of parents, and she gave me the name of a book she thought would help. At one point, she paused in her chopping to say, "I wonder what they talk about at racquetball," and we speculated on that for a minute. Soon the halibut, surrounded by herbs, tomatoes, and the shallots, was ready for baking. Broccoli for steaming was set out on the chopping block next to a loaf of French bread; the rice was measured, the salad ready, and two new candles were lit on the table in the dining area. The apartment, which had looked abandoned only a few minutes before, now looked lived-in and magically cozy. We moved into the living room, decorated in shades of mustard and dusty blue; the lighting was just right. And when Diane's husband, Joel, walked in and announced, the way Ricky Ricardo might have done in an old *I Love Lucy* episode, "Boy am I tired," Diane and I both started to laugh.

However, to compare my friends' marriage to Lucy and Ricky's, with Lucy's wide-eyed conniving and Ricky's blustery machismo, would be absurd. In fact, even the labels "husband" and "wife," as I've always thought of them, with the masculine and feminine roles and responsibilities they evoke, don't sound right. While my parents were married, my father was surely a husband, my mother a wife; their marriage, like most others I remember from childhood, seemed heavy with unexamined and mechanical dependencies. Joel and Diane instead are like two great pals but closer. Their dependence upon each other is not of the "where are my gloves, honey?" kind, but private—you can't see it at first glance. What they seem to be held together by are not the mechanics of marriage, as I've thought of them, but simply by love.

While Joel went to change out of his business clothes, I asked Diane why, on top of her job, she did the rest— the cooking, the shopping, the candles, the tidying up. "I do it," she said, "because I don't know how not to. Nobody's making me be a woman or a wife." But then she went on, and later I wondered whether she had confessed more than she meant to, or less: "My marriage is fine," she said. "I mean, it's not perfect, but I'm happy, even if I'm not doing it right, or equally. But the strange thing is that, close as we are, I thought marriage would be different—that it would be one 'thing' with two people inside. With us, it's more like two separate marriages, his and mine. Joel probably thinks he does half the work, but he doesn't. I don't think he knows what my side of the marriage is like. Half the time, talking to him is like talking to a can of soup—about my feelings, for one thing, or things I worry about at the office. He doesn't get it. He doesn't know. I guess," she concluded vaguely, "men are just different."

Though I'm not married myself, I knew right away and all too well what she meant. A few years ago, I would have been disheartened or angered by her comments, to say nothing of that scene at dinner— the stereotypical bustling women and the tired-and-hungry-husband-arriving-for-dinner, oblivious to the care and trouble that went into it. I would have argued that men don't have to be "different." After all, our generation, Diane's and mine, was out to prove that there need be no built-in distinctions between the sexes. We would share everything, fifty-fifty, from boardrooms and floor-waxing to the emotional "chores" of love, marriage, and family. For the first time in history, the motto of marriage was to be: Don't treat me like a "wife" and I won't treat you like a "husband." But now, since more of my friends have paired off and since I've been living with a man myself, I've had a better chance to know liberated men and women not on paper but in action, which is to say negotiating new and untried rules of equality—and making their inevitable private compromises in the name of love.

Off and on that evening, I thought about Diane's compromises, and, as Joel cleared the table, I tried to imagine how the marriage looked from his "side," the compromises or sacrifices he himself must have made, and whether he too would argue that women and men are "different." I tried to bring the subject up over coffee, but Diane glanced at me uneasily, and Joel and my boyfriend looked politely puzzled, as if I'd asked them a question in Chinese. Quickly, we switched to more general conversation and never returned to the question of why men and women are "different."

As I write this, relations between the sexes—on the surface at least—seem more troubled to me than ever before. *Divorce Court* reveals a terrible and different drama on TV every day. In the past year, there have been no fewer than three best-sellers about misogyny, variations on the theme of men hating women. Newspaper life-style pages report continually on the strains of two-career marriages and second marriages; the dilemma of whether to have children or not; the failure of old-fashioned marriages in new-fashioned times; of tensions that arise when the woman makes more money than the man (as 20 percent of working wives now do); and of the many adult relationships that fall apart before they even reach the prenuptial-agreement stage. When I hear friends despair over the 50-percent divorce rate and think about all that could possibly go wrong, I marvel instead at the marriages I've seen that do manage to succeed. And I marvel at the power of love, or if not love, at least what Dr. Johnson called the "triumph of hope over experience."

The experts have little in the way of good news to tell us. "Contrary to the common wisdom," says Letty Pogrebin in *Family Politics,* "married men are generally happier and healthier [!] than bachelors, but single women are happier and healthier [!] than married women." And yet married men are sexually unfaithful as much as 20 percent more than married women—who themselves are not exactly laggards in the infidelity department these days: One pessimistic estimate suggests that two out of three of all contemporary baby-boom marriages will be accompanied, from one side or the other, by an extramarital affair. If this prediction holds true, not only will we divorce more than our parents did, we'll also beat them at infidelity—we, the generation for whom equal partnerships, uncomplicated sexuality, and honest communication were supposed to be not a romantic ideal but the norm.

What's gone wrong? Can it really be that—despite all the much-deplored sexual inequality of the past—love, marriage, and family were nonetheless stable and trustworthy aspects of life all through history and are only now, for the first time, in terrible shape? Of course not. In the first place, the definitions of marriage, family, and even the role we expect love to play in our lives are not fixed but fluid; these definitions need revising with every generation. In the second place, liberation, as many men and women like Joel and Diane have seen at first hand, has its price—and the costs to love, marriage, and family can be painfully high. Is feminism to blame for the tensions today between men and women? Is the problem, as fundamentalist preachers insist, a widespread moral breakdown? Or are we facing something at once more mundane and more serious: Is the historic equilibrium between the sexes burdened now by an economy that forces men and women to compete for scarce resources in order to survive? There's no simple answer. But one explanation that makes sense to me comes from an odd source, for I wouldn't have thought that new research about the life cycle could tell us so much about men, women, and love.

Conventional postindustrial life-cycle wisdom has it that, for the most part, men and women go through life on parallel and complementary tracks, which intersect at mid-life and then run parallel again. As Erik Erikson, and others—from Carl Jung to Gail Sheehy— have outlined the adult life cycle, the healthy male would reach maturity, begin to define himself professionally, take on a wife, and start his family. At mid-life, having fought to earn a living for his family, he would see death around the corner and, for the first time, stop to take a look at the world. His so-called "feminine" qualities would emerge. Suddenly, his nurturing side would come out and possibly a newly discovered gentleness. He would no longer have to prove himself in the "masculine" realm; he could begin to express himself in a fuller, sensuous, more visibly open-hearted way, without threatening his manhood. The phrase "life begins at forty," for example, comes from a best-selling book by that title published during the Depression, which proposed that a man's happiest years would come after the struggles of early manhood. It's no coincidence that until now, men had tended to become more sentimental and loving as they aged—think of the man who is a more indulgent and demonstrative grandfather than he was a father, and not just because the child is someone else's direct responsibility.

A woman's life cycle took place on the other track. She would reach maturity, secure both her professional and personal identities vicariously through loving a man, and, once married, would assume the posture of wife and usually mother. In general, she had no separate identity but acquired her stature from those to whom she was connected, the way small children are braver when they're hanging onto their mothers' skirts. As she cared for her husband and family, however, she would deplete her nurturing instincts. At mid-life, her primary work completed, and her husband now more "feminine" in sensibility, she too would envision death and become more assertive, joining the outside world she had not been a part of until now. (Think of the age at which Betty Friedan became an active feminist—mid-life.) Having provided love and nurturing all these years, the woman was restless to find out about herself. Thus, at mid-life, men and women became more alike, as their rigorous gender differences mellowed, grew less important, and began to fade. The point to remember here is that this emotional merger could not have happened—or happened so dramatically—without the earlier enforced separation of the sexes by the roles each was expected to play.

There were always variations on these broad patterns, of course, and no one knows for certain whether they were culturally or physiologically determined, though it is known that men and women seem to "exchange" hormones sometime in mid-life, when estrogen and testosterone, the feminine and masculine hormones that determine sexual differences, diminish in women and men respectively, a decline which appears at least in part to effect these mid-life personality transformations. Hormones aside, though, what is more important is that the world has changed significantly since Jung, Erikson, and their followers recorded these conventional life-cycle assumptions. The men and women of the postwar generation no longer make their ways through life on these traditional parallel and complementary tracks: We're thrust instead, men and women together, onto the same track, traveling in a single train.

I say the "young men and boys" rather than the "young people" because the problems . . . belong primarily, in our society, to the boys: how to be useful and make something of oneself. A girl does not *have* to, she is not expected to, "make something" of herself. Her career does not have to be self-justifying, for she will have children, which is absolutely self-justifying, like any other natural or creative act. With this background, it is less important, for instance, what job an average young woman works at till she is married. . . .

—PAUL GOODMAN,
Growing Up Absurd

American girls did, and no doubt do, play down their intelligence, skills, and determinitiveness when in the presence of datable boys, thereby manifesting a profound psychic discipline in spite of their reputation for flightiness.

—ERVING GOFFMAN,
The Presentation of Self in Everyday Life

The comments above, from immensely successful books of their time, show how deeply influential Erikson's views of the life cycle were until our postwar generation came of age—with its new ideas about the roles of women and men, its uniquely high percentage of ambitious and educated women, and in a flailing economy where "woman's work" now includes coming up with half the rent. From the structure of the workplace to the rituals of dating, the premise, as every feminist will tell you, was the same: Women, at least in the first half of life, were to be responsible for making men's lives in the "real" world possible. What Goodman and Goffman are saying is that not only were women responsible for washing the socks and raising the kids—more important still was their role as psychological helpmates: Under the terms of the traditional life cycle, women's work was to give the men in their lives unqualified emotional space and support, to do everything possible to ensure that these men could live out their potential and their dreams. For women, there was only one legitimate dream. In exchange for money to buy laundry soap, women were expected to give up their names, their own dreams, and their souls to a man, his job, his house, and his children. And for all its drawbacks on both sides, this formula, in its way, worked for a long time: The life cycle was lived out much as it was laid out, as if Erikson's formulas were as much a biological imperative as the arrival of baby teeth or puberty.

Now consider the new life-cycle "formula" for men and women in the first half of life today: Upon reaching maturity—and we are the first generation for which this is so widely true—we do not complement each other so much as compete with each other, as we all, men and women alike, try to succeed, achieve autonomy, and find out who we are. Despite any superficial deference to the old formulas—like Diane's and Joel's—and whether we think about it or not, we're all competing in the marketplace for jobs and status—and, just as important, we're also competing for the emotional space and support that used to be a woman's most self-sacrificing gift to her man. We can no longer afford the accommodations to gender that men and women have made in the past: I don't know many women who would "play dumb" on a date or who dabble tentatively at a job, trusting that a husband will be along shortly, and I don't know many men who'd dare to present themselves anymore as sole kings of the castle. Most of us—literally—no longer make "gender deals" of the you-peel-the-carrots-and-I'll-pay-the-rent sort, or if we do, we negotiate them carefully; such deals are no longer almost automatic. Today, there are two people to contribute to the rent, two people who need the unqualified emotional support that pursuing a vocation or personal dream requires, and maybe no one to peel the damn carrots. Or to put it another way, in most relationships today, there are two adults with the same needs—Diane and Joel, for example—and no longer a man and woman whose separate needs justify a working, give-and-take balance.

"Gender characteristics," writes Alice Rossi, a former president of the American Sociological Association who has recently written on gender and the life cycle, "are clearly modifiable under changed social circumstances, as men and women take on either greater or lesser similarity of roles and experience. . . . Political and economic pressures are now blurring traditional gender roles in the first half of life." In other words, the postwar women Rossi refers to have had to subdue their loving, nurturing instincts for the sake of self-assertion—a stage which, in Erikson's day, wouldn't have emerged till mid-life. Similarly, to make sense of this new world, men have had to tap their feminine sensibilities, if only rhetorically—or if only by learning the pragmatics of ordering Chinese takeout for themselves—much earlier than they would have tapped them in the past.

It follows that once gender distinctions have begun to blur in the outside world, so too will they be transformed in the intimate worlds of love and marriage—inarguably crucial benchmarks of adulthood. Where once men and women "borrowed" inner resources from each other—a stoic man would put his arms around his crying wife, as if she were crying for both of them—now we strive ideally to cultivate inner resources of our own against any eventuality: Men are encouraged to learn to cry for themselves in much the same way that women have been encouraged to face the world apronless and head-on. Our expectations from love and marriage are high, even so, for to be-

lieve that men and women are not "different" is to expect complete understanding from a mate, to fail to
allow for the unknowable mysteries between people
and the sexes that in all likelihood make complete understanding too much to expect. We all have, as Virginia Woolf once said of women, our "own contrary
instincts."

If to be an adult now means to internalize all the
strengths and virtues of both sexes, it also means that
we've abandoned those you-peel-the-carrots-and-I'll-
pay-the-rent rules and roles of gender. Why then the
new strain on relationships? Shouldn't it have worked
out instead that, with some of the pressure off both
sides, love and marriage would be all the easier? Why is
my friend Diane unable to find the point, the center, of
her marriage? The answer is disquieting: In loving relationships that require neither "husbands" nor
"wives," where the traditional rules and roles have
been cast out, there's love and only love at the center.
If we don't need to borrow so freely anymore from
each other's strengths and resources, or to depend on
each other for rent and peeled carrots, our only need
for each other is our human, compelling, and unre-
lenting need for love. And love, of course, is a problem.

| 11 |

MARRIAGE

There was no getting out of it. My friends were getting married last summer in the South, at the bride's mother's home, and when the invitations went out over the phone, we guests were given not only the date but also our flight numbers, the name of the motel we'd all be staying in, and instructions to bring a bathing suit and plan to stay the weekend. Before I had a chance to think of an excuse, a more precise schedule followed: swimming upon arrival; dinner Friday night at a local restaurant with good southern food; late breakfast on Saturday; free time or sightseeing in the afternoon, followed by the ceremony and wedding supper; breakfast on Sunday; afternoon departure. I quickly called up another draftee I knew, to make sure she and her husband would be going. "'Command performance,'" she said. "Yeah, we're going." Reluctantly, we agreed that, much as we didn't

want to go hundreds of miles for a wedding, we
wouldn't want to miss it either.

There would be no more than thirty guests in all—
the bride's relatives and childhood friends, those of us
from New York, where the bride and groom had lived
for many years, and a few others flying in from such
places as Florida, Atlanta, Washington, even France.
We New Yorkers met at the airport, looking, as someone said, like first-timers off to "wedding camp." From
then on, wedding camp it was.

The bride and groom met our shift at the airport
and, barely pausing for greetings, ushered us into two
cars, drove us to the motel, saw us checked in, passed
out Xerox copies of handmade local maps (motel,
childhood home, and points of interest marked with an
X), and gave us each an agenda. Then they disappeared, promising to return soon to pick us up. As we
made our way to our rooms, I could tell I wasn't the
only one thinking that it might turn out to be a very
long weekend.

My friends were hardly starry-eyed beginners at
marriage. Both had been married before, and one
had teenage children from an earlier try. They had
been living together for a number of years, had had
their fair share of upsets, and knew, as far as anyone
can know, what lay ahead for them. I don't think that
they were looking forward to a rosy lifetime of bliss so
much as they were to sanctifying a familiar, abiding
love, as sturdy and comfortable as a pair of well-worn
jeans: They already knew their marriage would be
right for everyday wear and hoped it would hold up
with time, though they knew it would fade and inevitably require a few patches. Other friends of theirs had

asked me, "Why now? Why are they getting married *now*, after living together all this time?" I didn't know for sure. But I think my friends decided to marry publicly only after they knew they were already married privately in the deep, irrevocable ways that really matter.

Statistically speaking, we guests covered the late twentieth-century demographic gamut: There were single people among us, divorced men and women, a few others on their second or third marriages, and a pair of male lovers; there were parents and those of us without children. One couple had been debating marriage for a long time and, I thought, seemed to be watching the proceedings with nervous interest. When it came to weddings, we were not, to say the least, the most blushingly sentimental crowd ever assembled. Much as we all cared about the friends who had brought us together, it would take a lot to transform us from rowdy and skeptical wedding campers into awed and silenced witnesses to what is supposed to be the most sacred of ceremonies.

By Saturday, wedding camp seemed like home. We'd all met one another by then, and we northerners were beginning to get used to "y'all" and accept the southern hospitality that seemed exotic to us, with our "get it yourself" manners. We'd all followed the X to a good breakfast that morning, and then most of us had followed another X to the pool at the bride's family's house. It was a steaming hot day and, away from our usual rituals and obligations, we splashed around like children; the unlikeliest campers turned out to be terrific at a race someone invented in which you had to get from one end of the pool to the other by jumping. By late afternoon, when it was time to dress for the wedding, most of us had sunburnt noses.

The wedding was at six on Saturday in the garden of the family house, and it was still hot when we all gathered there fifteen or twenty minutes early. We were dressed up by then and solemn, no longer campers: Now we were waiting for the wedding.

While we waited, I watched the crowd. All these separate lives, I thought, and yet we are connected in our different ways to a man and woman about to marry: Over there were the bride's friends from her childhood and youth, her pretty mother and sisters, her niece and nephew. One of her sisters had made the wedding dress, which none of us had seen yet. There was the groom's close friend of twenty years, rehearsing a passage he was going to read from the Bible. Here were his children, themselves a big part of the marriage that would begin tonight. And there were the rest of us—despite the forced irony of the day before, awed witnesses after all. Soon a lone gospel singer began to sing "Amazing Grace," which always makes me cry, and before the ceremony had even begun, I wondered how I had been so stupid or cynical as to have forgotten to bring Kleenex.

My friends had had a hard time finding the right minister to express what they hoped their marriage would mean to them. Many services start from the unvarying and unrealistic premise that the bride and groom are embarking upon life as if for the first time, and that marriage itself will be the foundation for that life. This was not the case here. This bride and groom had pasts and ghosts and they weren't starting with clean slates; they had survived the pain of earlier failed marriages, and they were celebrating that survival, the future, and a love to which life is no stranger.

Finally, they found a minister who knew about love set in the real world. He knew that a marriage doesn't thrive all by itself, and he honored the friends and family who were there, and especially the groom's children, now to be the bride's stepchildren; husband and wife would not be alone in their new life together. Delicately, he acknowledged the love that had brought my friends "this far," and called the wedding day not a day of fulfillment but a day of promise. Then he prefaced the vows with something he had written himself:

> For in a world grown accustomed to living apart, in a world accepting of the gulfs that divide us, in a broken world, the wedding day stands as a sign of hope. . . .
>
> Luther called marriage the "little church," because daily love bridges the gulf between two otherwise selfish creatures, daily self-sacrifice is needed, and daily forgiveness must be offered and received. . . .
>
> Marriage is the faith that another knows you and holds you. Marriage is the hope that as your life unfolds, it will not be lonely. Marriage is the love whose discipline and commitment bear joy and wonder. This is indeed a time of promise. . . .

I don't know: For my part, and like many of my contemporaries, maybe I've protected myself too long and too well against marriage. I've told myself that marriage is less important now, a faltering institution, unsure of its place late in this confusing century, in this broken world. I've tried to make myself believe it's

unnecessary or obsolete, like corsets and manual type-
writers. In the same broken world, however, my
friends had found happiness in each other and made
that happiness public and sacred with their promises:
Isn't that the point?

In colonial New England, when a couple decided to
marry, a notice was posted outside the church, and by
law everyone in the colony, from the governor on
down, was required to donate at least a few ears of
corn to get the marriage off to the right start. This
seems overly generous for the notoriously parsimon-
ious Yankees—until you consider how important marriage and family were to the young colonies. The
Yankees were thrifty, but they weren't stupid: It was
essential to them that every colonist be settled into a
family, not only to populate the New World in an organized way but also because the larger community had
neither the time nor the resources to be charitable to
odd men and women out.

To take an obvious example, there were no hospitals
in colonial New England; it was the family's job to tend
to the sick. Nor were there insurance companies. Families did what could be done to mop up after a tragedy.
Families took care of their own then, the way we now
rely on nursing homes for the old, shelters for the
homeless, schools for the young, and counseling for
the troubled. Where early New Englanders would arrange barn raisings, now we'd apply to a bank for a
mortgage. Where the colonists were wise to glorify the
family as a necessary, productive, and self-sufficient institution, now there are outside institutions—everything from computer dating, the Yellow Pages, and

summer camps to fire departments and the Supreme Court—to maintain the social order and service the family's and community's needs. If the family once was the vital social and economic link *to* the outside world, today there's no escaping the outside world's intrusions. Now it's the family's primary role to offer a stable emotional and domestic haven *from* the unstable world outside.

Thus, over the past few centuries of industrialization, marriage and family have evolved naturally from the practical to the emotional centers of our lives, as increasingly we develop autonomous, self-reliant identities out in the world—and come home to rest, as it were, and to be restored by the love of our partners or families. Technically speaking, my friends who married last summer didn't *need* to marry, not in the sense the colonists did. Both are self-supporting. Both have dependable friends and family. For years, they had been living together, and without moral qualms or social ostracism. Their need to marry had to do with longings for permanence, tradition, for a contract more binding than a lovers' agreement—vague reasons to marry but compelling, nonetheless. As another friend of mine explains her recent decision to marry, "To me, marriage is like the story of the Three Little Pigs. When I was single, I felt like the pig who lived in the straw house, vulnerable. Now I feel like I live in the brick house." (Her husband's reasons are less vivid, if no less sentimental: "It was like saying in a church that you'd be there for each other," he says, "and I wanted that.") Not that marriage is impervious to huffing, puffing, betrayal, or disappointment—but marriage, as both friends would probably agree, is working to make the illusion of a brick house the closest thing possible to a safe and permanent haven.

Marriage for the New Englanders and, as we've seen, even for my parents' generation, was based on widely accepted, clear-cut roles, responsibilities, and expectations. For my contemporaries and me, on the other hand, marriages are based on abstract and harder-to-realize longings for what family life might, with luck, do for the soul. According to *Habits of the Heart,* "The more love and marriage are seen as sources of rich psychic satisfactions, it would seem, the less firmly they are anchored in an objective pattern of roles and social institutions. . . . If love and marriage are seen primarily in terms of psychological gratification, they may fail to fulfill their older social function of providing people with stable, committed relationships that tie them into the larger society." And what makes marriage so difficult today is that these new expectations of ours are elusive: What's a metaphorical brick house? How, precisely, do you define being there? It's easy to tell when the expectations are not being met, harder to tell when they are.

To put it another way, what these authors of *Habits* are suggesting is that most of us have to be our own anchors today. It's not the role of marriage to "tie" us into the world, as most of us would perceive it. Instead, what we hope for most from our loving relationships is that two anchors will hold better than one: Love, we hope, will fill up our empty spaces and give us the strength and confidence to go on with our own lives, so that we can feel safer, be happier and more comfortable together in love or marriage than we could on our own. Not that there aren't practical reasons to marry—

two paychecks, and if there are to be children, two parents are also better than one. Even so, marriage and family work for us when we're happy, when his, her—and their—emotional needs are met. For the colonists and, to a lesser extent, most subsequent generations until our own, the ideal of happiness was scarcely the highest priority of family life. Love was optional, less important for most people than food, clothing, shelter, and "suitability."

Yet the legacy of the essential marriage—for survival, for the social order, for the soul—is with us still. No matter that we talk of the death of the family, the 50-percent divorce rate. There remains something exalted, almost mystical, about a marital bed, a child born to husband and wife, the family home, sharing a history, building a life together. For most of us, a happy, successful marriage still dominates our dreams. I've always thought it one of our more curious customs, for example, that when a child comes of age and leaves home to set up adult housekeeping, almost ritualistically the child's parents will search the attic or garage to offer the fledgling adult their broken dishes, long-discarded furniture, gifts of the family junk. If the child should go on to live with a lover, the parents mark the passage usually by worrying. But if the same child gets married, that's another story, a rite of passage worth celebrating. Out goes the old stuff. Not only parents, but friends, relatives, even business associates are expected to come up with fine gifts to assure the couple a bountiful start in their new life together, not so different a custom from that of the colonists' offerings of corn. For all the changes we've seen in the structure of the family and for all the new possibilities for living a full life on one's own, in some ways even today it's as if "real" life, "real" adulthood doesn't begin until marriage.

When I think about marriage, what I long for most, strangely enough, is not an elevated spiritual union with a man; that's a fantasy not readily envisioned. What seems wondrous to me instead are the small, shared rituals that bind a man and woman in familiar intimacy, the borders inside which they make love, choose furniture, plan vacations, quarrel over closet space, share the toothpaste, celebrate Christmas the same way they did last year. I've been in love myself, so I know something of what it's like to build a life together—the private jokes, the friends you share, knowing in advance which of you makes the coffee and which goes for the paper, even the comfortable tedium of hearing his or her favorite story yet again. To promise to share forever the small—not only the grand—moments of life seems to me profoundly human, more intimate even than making love with someone for the first time.

I'm also touched by how binding these small rituals can be, how universal and timeless the pull toward cozy dependency, no less a comfort to us today than it was to the colonists, or to my parents when they were happy together. What seems to me new about marriage is not the idea that you can find peace in domestic stability, but that this kind of stability can also be a springboard for freedom: What's new is the idea that marriage can help you in the push for autonomy. A generation ago, most men and women felt duty-bound to squeeze their characters into a fixed idea of marriage. As a man who married in the late fifties told a reporter: "All I did was go out and work all day. All she did was stay home and clean house. It was really very stifling, but I sort of assumed that was marriage." Today it's up to the marriage to fit the partners, not the other way around.

In one marriage I know of, neither husband nor wife could decide who should make the bed. Their solution was to buy a big comforter, and whoever sleeps later throws it haphazardly over the sheets and other blankets. As a matter of principle, the bed never gets made. I met a man recently who'd been married for four years—happily, he says—and even though he and his wife live in a perfectly ample condominium, he'd held on to the lease of the scruffy apartment he'd had when he was single. "I just like the privacy of going there sometimes," he says.

When I first heard of commuter marriages some years ago, I wondered how a man and woman could sustain intimacy over long weeks apart. Now I know of several such marriages, and by all accounts they work—"much better than when we were together all the time," a commuting wife told me cheerfully. Many presumably happily married men and women I know have lives so separate they barely overlap. Other marriages are complicated by stepchildren, ex-wives, ever-present old boyfriends, or other demands from the past that make marriage in the present more complicated to juggle. How, with no roadmaps and against all likely odds, some of these marriages work so well I'll never know, but how thrilling to see such an apparently immovable institution submit to scrutiny and revision and, sometimes at least, emerge intact.

It is sometimes said that marriages go through predictable cycles of peace, turmoil, and change, but as I've watched friends of mine work their way into marriage, I've come to doubt this. It seems to me that a man and woman who marry at twenty-one will have a marriage different from what they would have if they'd married at thirty. Second marriages, marriages with or without children, marriages between people who endure tragedies, marriages that have to weather severe career disruptions on one or both sides—isn't every marriage unique, at least in some respects? At every point along the life cycle, it makes sense that the emotional variables—his needs, her needs, their needs together—will change. To suggest that all marriages will follow the same route is to suggest that all people are more or less the same, too, and I suspect that's how marriage got into trouble in the first place; its very unpredictability is what makes marriage such an awesome commitment. To expect a marriage to go through predictable crises is to invite disappointment: The unpredictable crises are likelier to make or break a marriage.

Just in the past month, I heard about the sad divorce of a friend, but I also read in the paper the wedding announcements of two other people I know; for some at least, the urge to consecrate love is as persistent and human as the compulsion to survive. I like to think about getting married myself one day: It would be a small wedding—but a big marriage, honest, with plenty of room to move around, room perhaps for children, and somehow a good deal of privacy. It would be the kind of marriage described in a 1933 guide to the subject, which said, "Let's face the bitter truth. Not many of us are born lovers, or great lovers, or tireless, congenital, chronic lovers. We are normal people, feeble, fumbling, well-meaning, bewildered and lonely in the crowd of the world. What we really want is a friend or two, and a companion who will be glad when we are glad, sorry when we are sorry, stick to us in adversity, and last the course."

| 12 |

MAINTENANCE OF THE WORLD

One day last winter, a month or so after I'd turned thirty-five and was worrying more than usual about whether I'd ever have a child, I dragged a skeptical friend with me to an animal shelter to adopt a dog. "Are you sure you know what you're doing?" he asked me over and over. "Do you know how a dog can tangle up your life?" No, I didn't know; no, I wasn't sure. "Of course I'm sure," I said.

The dogs at the shelter can sense right away why you've come. They straighten up in their cages, heads tilted appealingly. It must be their survival strategy to look you right in the eye, begging to be chosen—but with a heartrending, self-protective reserve and dignity about it; I couldn't bear to meet their gazes. In a panic, I began to think of all the really good reasons why I shouldn't adopt a dog (city apartment, irregular schedule, too much responsibility), and how I could possibly explain my sudden change of heart to the helpful volunteer. My friend's hands were clenched into fists at his sides, as though he were restraining himself from grabbing a couple of leashes and making a run for it. He looked at me accusingly. Leaving empty-handed was out of the question.

Phil, as I would later call him, was outside playing with several other dogs in a fenced-in yard, and I first saw him from a distance: a wiry blond of complex lineage, hair falling in his eyes, paws that sort of turn out, and a peculiar red nose. Unlike the others, he didn't seem to care whether I adopted him or not. The volunteer told me that he had been to obedience school, but was vague about telling me that he had flunked it. By then, it didn't matter. I could already picture myself taking Phil for walks, teaching him tricks, having him curl up at my feet, a loving, real-life hot-water bottle I could love in return. "I will never dog-sit, so don't ever ask," said my friend.

Phil will not play with dog toys, I would learn, or eat dog biscuits, though he likes bagels and cream cheese. His hunting instinct gets the better of him sometimes, and he hunts by tipping over wastebaskets. Should he happen to find a bone in one, he will bury it—in the nearest bed. He comes when called, but then runs away again. He knows no tricks. I had expected him to comfort me, as I'd known other dogs to do. Instead, if I cry, Phil trots off in mild annoyance to where it's quieter, refusing to be bothered. He won't bark when strangers come near, but barks at thunderstorms and the wind. He's not an easy dog. Yet my heart went out to him forever one night shortly after I'd gotten him, when he saw himself in a large framed mirror waiting to be hung that was leaning against a wall at a friend's house. Phil looked at himself in the mirror, turned sideways, looked away, and looked again, thinking over this new puzzle. Then he peered curiously behind the mirror, as if to greet the other dog who had to be hiding there.

A few months later, in the spring, I lured Phil into my boyfriend's station wagon. We were in the country, and we were going garden shopping, for some white rosebushes. As we packed them into the car, Phil leaped without warning out of the back of the wagon, onto a crowded two-lane highway. There was no way to stop him. Cars began to swerve; you could hear a dozen horns at once. I saw Phil, crouched and looking half his size, dart somehow to the safety of the meadow across the highway. My boyfriend had turned away in shaken horror, unwilling to watch Phil die. I didn't think about him dying. I didn't move. I just watched; maybe I thought I could save him with my eyes. Even Phil was subdued on the way home.

I wasn't shaken at the time, but hours later I was: How could I have been so sure he wouldn't die, I asked myself. How could I have been so presumptuous? That I wasn't used to death, didn't expect it, seemed a shallow excuse. Of course he could have died, this dependent creature I had agreed to care for and come to love. Animals die in the streets all the time. And what if he hadn't been a dog—that was bad enough—but a child, a child in my care, the child I often dream about having? How can you make good on your promise to keep a child alive?

It would be too easy to say that I was transformed forever by Phil's near-accident, that I saw life more clearly because my dog was almost killed. I have noticed, though, that I really do think more about death now than I used to, which is another way of saying that I think more about life, my own life and the ways in which it touches others', or doesn't. I watch over Phil, and I worry about friends who travel on holiday weekends. I have a young niece now, and I want her to be safe. I worry about my parents, not yet old, and I worry about people I don't even know—abandoned children, lonely victims of AIDS, the homeless. This is not to imply that I've become saintly or unaccustomedly generous; my idle worrying amounts to very little. Increasingly, however, I'm aware of a new, unfocused, but almost physical need I have to disseminate my soul. It's a hunger for the rewards of giving and loving selflessly, a need to be needed. Perhaps I'm talking about nothing more than the usual maternal impulses, or a side effect of my biological clock ticking too fast; but the evidence suggests that what I'm feeling is universal.

It occurs to me that this recent restlessness of mine, this need to set boundaries and protect my corner of the world, coincides uncannily with what many experts predict will happen to all of us at about my stage in the life cycle: I must be feeling what they think of as the natural, human longing to be the "hero" of my life, to justify my existence, to reach for immortality. Caring for Phil, wanting a child, maybe writing this book, and in various other ways, I must be doing what we all must do to become adult, to prove we're human, to prove that our own reality connects in a meaningful way with others' and won't simply die when we do: I must be trying to make an offering to the world in recompense for what the world has offered me.

The whole thing boils down to this paradox: If you are going to be a hero then you must give a gift.

—ERNEST BECKER,
The Denial of Death

Unlike many Americans I know, men and women who love to speculate about children (will I ever have them? do I want them? will I get my life together in time to have one? what would I do with one? what would become of me without one?), my British friend Julia is impatient with the subject. She's in her forties, once divorced and once widowed, and now she lives in a beautiful house alone with her dog, surrounded by friends, and godchildren and relatives who visit occasionally; she has a demanding business of her own, and is often involved in community projects. I'm a little awed by how serene she seems, how much she seems to get done, and I've always thought privately what a good mother she would have made. One night I asked her why she hadn't had children. "Oh, you poor American girls," she said; "all that pressure to have children. You think there's something wrong with you if you don't."

She went on to describe her childhood in postwar England, where an extreme shortage of men (many more British soldiers than Americans had been killed in the War) had left a lot of women single. I knew something about this: There was, for example, no postwar baby boom in England. Since her parents had had to travel extensively for their work, she was often left in the care of friends and relatives, sometimes married couples with or without children, and sometimes in the care of single women, whom she much preferred.

"These ladies," she said, "were free and happy, and they could do what they wanted. I guess the role models who impressed me most were those women. Everybody else I stayed with seemed tired all the time. I knew I wanted to be more like the ladies, do different kinds of things. I thought about having children—a lot—and might have done. Finally, it was my decision not to. But I never felt I had to apologize for it."

In contrast, I began to think about myself and my other friends, and the baby mania that seems to me now in the air (probably because of my getting-close-to-the-wire age), and the lengths men and women will go to these days to reproduce—freezing sperm, hiring surrogate mothers, going thousands of miles to adopt a child, enduring amniocentesis and painful tests and operations to improve upon one's fertility odds. Men and women of my generation did not grow up with a variety of role models from which to choose, the way my British friend did; as we've seen, parenthood a generation ago was virtually synonymous with adulthood. Especially for women, in particular women in their late twenties and thirties who want children and who have until now, either by choice or by accident, put careers ahead of family, the pressure to have children "in time" is no less urgent (if more painful) than the built-in pressure to get one's Christmas shopping finished before the deadline. Raising a child, as Becker says, is to give "the gift that society specifies in advance," the natural way to become the hero of your life, justify your existence, and assure yourself immortality—all at once. But now that having children is neither so simple nor so automatic a rite of passage as it once was, for many of us at least, this traditional express route to heroism and immortality, if indeed that is what it is, has to be reexamined.

Sometime in mid-life, according to Erik Erikson, in order to become adult we all must achieve what he calls "generativity": We have to help establish and guide the next generation. To Erikson, generativity is the appropriate by-product of healthy intimacy, and becoming a parent is reaching a state of psychological, secular grace, affirming one's place on the human continuum. This concept—and I wish Erikson himself had written more about it—is central to adulthood, yet it raises many troubling questions: If the impulse toward generativity "strikes" in mid-life, for example, what about the men and women who have children during their twenties, as most men and women did almost by rote when Erikson coined the term shortly after World War II? Could it be that such parents fail to realize the philosophical weightiness of generativity? Does Erikson mean to say that mid-life parents are "better"? Because generativity as Erikson defines it is more a psychological passage than a physiological one, why does the mid-life onset of generativity converge with a woman's mid-life biological decline in fertility? Couldn't nature have given women—as well as men—a little more time to act upon their generative impulses? And if Erikson was isolating generativity as primarily a male phenomenon, which he has been accused of having done, then can you ignore the fact that for many childless women, the biological/social panic over their childlessness occurs today at the very age when Erikson's psychological generativity crisis is scheduled to take place?

And what about bad parents, or selfish parents? Erikson concedes that the mere act of having a child is hardly enough to assure generativity: How good a parent does one have to be? Can one achieve a kind of generativity in reverse, where the decision not to bring a child into this world is one's "gift"? If generativity is humanity's way of replenishing the world's resources, then couldn't one argue that, given the state of the world's resources today, every child not born is as much a gift as every child born? Couldn't a woman who submits to an abortion because she can't make a life for her child be performing a generative act? And how can we reconcile to generativity those of us who would like to have children but can't or won't be able to? Is Erikson saying that we'll never achieve generativity, adulthood? Is he saying that my British friend, with her rich, full life, her useful work, and her community service, will never be fully human? Is he saying that Mother Teresa isn't a grown-up? Or that Jesus wasn't?

There's a qualifying clause in Erikson's first mention of generativity, which might easily have escaped notice during the baby-boom frenzy in which it first appeared, when raising children seemed as natural an act as breathing. Today, on the other hand, with more of us destined never to have children, this qualifier is crucial: "There are individuals," he writes, "who, through misfortune or because of special and genuine gifts in other directions, do not apply this drive [of generativity] to their own offspring. And indeed, the concept of generativity is meant to include such more popular synonyms as *productivity* and *creativity*. . . ." Or to put it another way, the child doesn't necessarily make the man or woman. In the largest sense possible, generativity is the impulse to altruism, no matter what the means.

About twenty-five years after he wrote the above, in 1974 and in a vastly different world, Erikson gave a series of lectures which were published as a book called *Dimensions of a New Identity*, and in which he reasserted the importance of generativity—but hinted that its achievement could be interpreted still more expansively:

> I must add that as a principle [generativity] corresponds to what in Hinduism is called the maintenance of the world, that middle period of the life cycle when existence permits you and demands you to consider death as peripheral and to balance its certainty with the only happiness that is lasting: to increase, by whatever is yours to give, the good will and the higher order in your sector of the world. That, to me, can be the only adult meaning of that strange word *happiness*. . . .

Maintenance of the world. To increase, by whatever is yours to give, the good will and the higher order in your sector of the world.

I know a man with an uncommon appreciation of nature who once, in the unlikely setting of a lively dinner party, told me a story I've never forgotten. He was traveling in Africa when someone gave him an orphaned infant monkey to hold; his heart went out to the wonder and helplessness of this tiny creature in a way that almost frightened him, and that he could describe only as maternal. He said he felt a stirring literally in his breasts to feed and protect the monkey, and the sensation moved him in a way that was different from the paternal stirrings he'd felt as a loving father many times before. In that transcendent moment, he came as close as he ever would to knowing what it would be like to bear and nurse a child. That rare knowledge took his breath away. His awareness—together with many other works and acts that have made his life passionate, spiritual, and good—is what I think of now when I think of generativity.

I think, too, of another friend, a woman who wants a child more than any other woman I've ever met. For years, she has undergone every sort of fertility treatment imaginable, without success. Still, her longings clearly go beyond simply wanting a child of her own for all the right or wrong reasons, for she spends time at a local hospital, where she's a volunteer nurturer who holds and feeds and soothes babies born to drug-addicted mothers and who are otherwise alone, awaiting their parents' return or suitable foster care.

Then there's the philanthropist who turns up in the New York papers all the time, bestowing trust funds on victims of terrible tragedies; one has rarely seen his picture, nor does he want publicity. True artists offer as their gifts their art, and many other vocations—medical research, social work—demand a selflessness and devotion that surely qualifies as generative. On a smaller scale, if altruism is relative, there are those people who are loyal friends, helpful neighbors, teachers or mentors, guiding the next generation along. Or my friend who tends his garden as gently as he would raise a child. The garden is spectacular, his gift, and he often opens it to the public, allowing it to be littered, plucked, and trampled, for charitable causes. Maintenance of the world.

Next to some of these gifts, my own self-serving and romantic fantasies of loving and raising a child seem downright stingy, not a gift at all. She (he?) would of course be beautiful, clever—no, brilliant, adoring, and would never turn into a sulky, demanding teenager. For my part, I would avoid all temptations to make my child too competitive (children born today will not have to compete in the way their baby-boom parents did, for they'll be a much smaller generation), or to turn him (her?) into the person I wish I'd become (a pianist?). In my fantasies, I'm fiercely certain that I could protect this child from the awful things our children are exposed to so early today, and that I could manage everything else in my life so that there'd be plenty of time simply to love this child. The fact that I've never met as good a mother as I'd be doesn't bother me in the least, except when I put the fantasy aside, and consider the risks and difficulties of raising a child selflessly, of giving any kind of gift at all. If generativity, however it expresses itself, combines awareness with the commitment to meaningful altruistic action, then surely it must be the central and most satisfying challenge of adulthood, of being human. No wonder Erikson wrote about it in a tone of reverence. No wonder it's so hard to achieve.

I'm at the age now where I have a growing collection of photographs of friends' and relatives' young children, and have seen generativity in action in the faces of new mothers and fathers humbled by the miracle of their own offspring. I'm at the age, too, where other friends are resigned or relieved to have put the question of reproducing aside. Sometimes they're too old now; other times they've just decided no to children for their own reasons. I've watched them turn to other causes, other passions, for the "good will and higher order of their sector of the world." I don't know yet where such impulses as I have will find their outlet, what (aside from Phil) my gift will be. I suppose some lucky people know what they want to give from the beginning, others search for a long time, and still others never find it. But there's a need for all sorts of gifts, and there'll be time to find one; it's not as if we're shopping for a world that already has everything.

| 13 |

THE CYCLE

It's a little like some tiny cave-in,
in my brain. There's a sense
that I've lost—not everything,
not everything, but far too much.
A part of my life forever.

—RAYMOND CARVER, "Hominy and Rain"

It's not really my garden, but because I've been planting and tending it for more than seven years, I like to
think of it as mine. It's a big garden, bordered at one
end with century-old boxwoods and at the other with a
small grove of lilacs, and largely shaded, so that the
predominant color is green, all shades of green, and
the flowers are pastel and not the brighter colors that
thrive only in full sun. There are bleeding hearts, as-
tilbe, roses, phlox, foxglove, daylilies in cream and ap-
ricot, columbine, ferns, Solomon's seal, and other

perennials whose names I can never remember, plus bulbs in the spring and bushes whose leaves turn bright red and gold in the fall, when the big snowball-like hydrangea blossoms are themselves turning a caramel brown.

The garden belongs to the man I've been seeing all this time, and was tended before me by his good friend, a woman who knows more about gardening than I probably ever will, and who was happy to turn it over to me because the pressures of her career were leaving her less and less time for all the care this big plot requires. So I bought some overalls and took up a trowel not long after this man and I entered each other's lives. Because relationships in the beginning are so tentative, and also because when I started I knew absolutely nothing about gardening, I began slowly. First I planted forget-me-nots and a heather, because I liked their romantic sound. The bushy heather is still there, and the forget-me-nots have jumped around and spread out, as plants will when they can. Every May, the mounds of ice-blue flowers bloom at the same time the deeper-shaded violets and stalky-purple ajuga come out, so that there's a moment each year when the garden seems all blue and purple and is, I think, at its prettiest, though others prefer it in April, when it's marsh-marigold yellow or later, in July, when the little white platycodon, called balloon flowers, are popping open, just one or two each day, and when the roses and lilies are at their best.

Work starts in the garden on the first warm day in mid-March; by now I know to weed and cultivate and fertilize the different beds in a certain order, determined by which beds will be hardest to squeeze into

later on, once the plants grow full. I lug around enor-
mous bags of peat moss and fall almost into a trance,
turning over the still-cold dirt. I like myself in the
garden, where the flowers seem pleased to have me
around and where I can feel at the same time strong
and gentle. And it's here that, over these past years, I
think I've begun to learn something about growing up.

My relationship with the garden's owner was a happy
one, and after a while I felt completely at home with
him. The house is his country house, a two-hour drive
from the city (when there's no traffic), and before long
we'd built a wonderful new life together there. It
seemed magical to me the way our love reached out to
our friends and could also be so private: Together and
apart, our lives worked in much the way I've tried to
describe adulthood in this book. We had strong separate selves, good times together, work we cared about,
friends, our separate families. Ours was a life made up
of seemingly small daily rituals that really stand for
much more: We'd cook together and entertain, and
take little walks into the village or longer walks in
nearby nature preserves. I usually won at backgam-
mon, but nobody could do crossword puzzles the way
he could. We learned to share the household tasks
pretty fairly—though he's the better cook—and with
respect to our work, we had a lot in common. Our life
was social, but the best times for me were the Friday-
night suppers we'd often have alone, in the kitchen by
the fireplace there, and when we'd talk, sometimes, till
bedtime.

The years blended together until they seemed to me
like a lifetime. I could feel myself becoming a woman,
no longer the girl I was when I met him, less shy,

bolder, and for a long time I thought I had brought out the best in him, too. But neither of us was perfect, of course. We had the kinds of disagreements people have today, but we always decided in the end that "things" would work out because we loved each other. And then it began to seem for the first time that perhaps things wouldn't work out after all. We began the long, back-and-forth process of breaking up. Now it's months later, and the breakup is still inconclusive, like life. Neither one of us seems able to say yes or no to forever.

I've stayed on in the house to finish this book, and how odd it's been to do my grieving alone in a house that now is haunted for me. The relationship began its decline in the fall, with more sadness than anger (though inevitably there was a lot of that, too), and as usual I began to prepare the garden for winter, cutting the beds back ruthlessly to the ground. It seemed right, or in the interest of an emotional symmetry I imagined to be right, that I should plant the bulbs for spring, the way I always had. The relentlessness of nature—that my bulbs would come up whether I was there or not—was not lost on me, and I procrastinated over their planting, until the nights grew colder and I had to bring the bulbs I'd bought inside, for fear they'd freeze. Usually after I begin planting, I become so excited by picturing how the tulips and daffodils and crocuses will look in the spring that I buy dozens more, in a happy excess of extravagance. I didn't do that this year, so next spring's showing will be comparatively spare. The final bulbs didn't go in until Thanksgiving weekend, at the last minute, but because it was a mild autumn the ground was still warm and easily turned.

What appeals to me most about the garden is the predictability of its cycles: With practice you know— more or less and barring the whims of nature—what will happen every month, and what the garden expects from its keeper all year long; it seems to tug at my shirttails when it needs to be weeded or watered, the way a child would signal that she wanted her lunch. It's a cycle where death promises lush renewal, unlike our own human life cycle in which constant renewal is what keeps death at bay for as long as we live.

I wonder what will happen to "my" garden if I'm not there next year; will someone else show the same favoritism to the billowy hosta and the fragrant sweet woodruff that I, secretly, always did? And if I remain, what will happen? Or will I have another garden one day, somewhere else? I don't know, of course; no one knows. But what I do know is that I never expected to "end up" here, in a life that has already had more pleasures and sorrows than I'd anticipated, in a life that seems no less unsettled than it ever was. I had mistakenly thought that life was indeed supposed to end up somewhere—most likely, or so I thought when I was younger, it would happen by age thirty or so. But life doesn't end up anywhere till it ends, which I suppose is the point.

The columnist Walter Lippmann once pointed out that the child holds onto things by grasping them, while an adult holds on by remembering and understanding them. A child, for example, will contrive to remember his vacation at the beach by returning home with a collection of chipped clamshells and sea-faded stones. The adult will keep the vacation alive in his memory—the sounds, the smells, the indelible picture of the child gathering his priceless souvenirs—and memory is enough. Such literary distinctions as Lippmann's I find wonderfully satisfying: Yes, I can say, I see what he means; and so I must know something of adulthood. But neither childhood nor adulthood is absolute. Stones and shells soon lose their evocative powers, and memory is especially tricky. It's likelier that we slip back and forth all our lives from the consciousness of an adult to that of a child, as we struggle to overcome our fears of the world and make peace with it. Lippmann himself also wrote: "For some parts of our personalities may well be more mature than others; not infrequently we participate in the enterprises of an adult with the mood and manners of a child."

My generation has not followed an orderly path into adulthood, either by our "mood and manners" or by accepting without question the roles and values proscribed by the culture into which we were born—but then, the world into which we were born wasn't the same world that greeted us as adults. Our life cycle is unfolding differently from those of the generations who came before us. We haven't chosen careers, married, bought houses, had children and then stumbled into mid-life crises in a specific, linear order, the way our parents seem to have done with such atypical regularity. We are not a generation who can easily measure our progress against that of our contemporaries, for there are many life-agendas now to choose from (or happen into), and many ways to express adulthood. No one, finally, can speak for us all.

The oldest among us is over forty now, and at a friend's fortieth birthday party I was recently asked when we're supposed to begin preparing for our mid-life crises, for middle age. Middle age! I hadn't thought about it, really. But is that the next step? Could it be that we'll just plunge into middle age like lemmings, our younger brothers and sisters following shortly behind us, over the cliff and into a sea of anxious regret or complacency?

The experts are divided on the subject: One places the mid-life crisis—that stage, or moment of life in which a profound awareness of the certainty of death makes us reevaluate the lives we've built in early adulthood—between thirty-five and forty-five; another between forty and forty-five, and others say that it can occur even later. Middle age, a more amorphous term describing that part of life between productive adulthood and old age, has been said by another expert to last until age sixty-four—confusing, arbitrary numbers. Will our own postwar generation transform these passages just as we altered the expectations of adolescence and young adulthood? Can we find a way to postpone the next stage? And should we want to?

Middle age became a "problem" stage of life only in this century and as a result of the increased average life expectancy, which in 1900 was around forty-eight or fifty. Before then, many parents had not lived to see their children out of adolescence; you avoided the "empty-nest syndrome" by dying. Vigorous adulthood, or the so-called "prime of life," and old age, if one lived that long, were contiguous. But as more and more people began living longer, as women lived to see their children make adult lives for themselves and men to see younger workers replace them as their energies declined, there came to be a kind of limbo age, when one was neither young nor old. More to the point, middle age had no function, the way young adulthood or even venerated old age did; to be middle-aged was to be without purpose.

But now, a century later, we're living a quarter of a century longer, on the average. We've stretched out adolescence, and young adulthood. We're marrying later, and we've added on to the number of years for safe childbearing. We're "younger" longer, and our productive years need have no predetermined deadline. The workplace has been restructured to include women, and the retirement age, which didn't exist a century ago, inches up as men and women remain vital much longer. As we age as a society—and our median age, which was sixteen in 1790, is now over thirty—we pay more attention to the ways in which old age can be rewarding. To ask when middle age begins is to ask when uselessness begins, when it's time to count the days till old age. And that depends on how we live our lives. The answer, one hopes, is never.

This is not to say that it's possible or desirable to ignore the passage of time, or to put off thoughts of death forever. Knowledge of death electrifies life with its meaning, and the perennial undertone of sadness that comes from realizing that death is out there somewhere is what makes us wise. A child's joy—over a toy, or a birthday cake—is momentary, and followed as often as not by no less momentary tears. An adult's joy is weighted with experience, however, and the tears that may accompany it know as much of compassion and sorrow as they do of joy. They are not tears to be taken lightly.

And when does adulthood, this awareness of death

in life sink in? At thirty-five? Forty-two? Thirty-eight?
Fifty-six? I don't know. I don't think such spiritual
awareness is something you learn once, at a certain
age, like multiplication tables. Its depths can't be measured. If the body ages predictably, I'm not sure the
same can be said for the mind, which is not so easily
governed by rules and which grows more wondrous
and mysterious the more we question it. Henry James,
decidedly not a scientist, believed that learning to live
takes a lifetime, "which is absurd, if there's not to be
another in which to apply the lessons." And V. S.
Pritchett wrote at age eighty that he had been "far, far
younger in my thirties than I had been in my twenties,
because my heart was fuller at thirty, my energies knew
their direction. . . ." His age—and he did not mean
chronological age—had always gone "up and down,"
depending. And at eighty he also wrote: "I suppose I
am slowly growing up."

NOTES ON SOURCES

I've tried to demonstrate in this book that it's fruitless to think about adulthood without taking into account the social, political, and economic conditions that shape the adult's world; as these conditions change, so, invariably, will the definition of adulthood. I was lucky to find a number of books that convinced me that this is so and, while these sources might be quoted from time to time in the text, such occasional references can't possibly reflect the number of times I turned to them for guidance. These books include Peter Laslett's *The World We Have Lost* (New York: Charles Scribner's Sons, 1965) and Lawrence Stone's *The Past and the Present* (Boston, London, and Henley: Routledge & Kegan Paul, 1981), both of which—though neither claims to be about adulthood—review the history of Western man's belief in his own powers. Joseph F. Kett's *Rites of Passage: Adolescence in America 1790 to the Present* (New York: Basic Books, Inc., Publishers, 1977) has as its thesis that youth is a shifting, nonfixed stage of life. Erik H. Erikson edited and introduced a provocative anthology called *Adulthood* (New York: W. W. Norton Co., 1978), which looks at the subject from many angles and suggests that "the archives for the study of adulthood still wait to be created"—which obviously I found heartening.

Habits of the Heart: Individualism and Commitment in American Life (Berkeley, Los Angeles, London: University of California Press, 1975), by Robert N. Bellah, Richard Madsen, William M. Sullivan, et al., covers much the same ground as I do; I found my own sensibilities and those of my friends brought to life repeatedly in this book. Barbara Ehrenreich's *The Hearts of Men: American Dreams and the Flight from Commitment* (Garden City, New York: Doubleday/Anchor Press, 1983) taught me why men are the way they are today, and Carol Gilligan's *In a Different Voice: Psychological Theory and Women's Development* (Cambridge, Massachusetts: Harvard University Press, 1982) taught me the same about women. As for understanding the baby-boom generation, I was impressed with Landon Y. Jones's *Great Expectations: America and the Baby-Boom Generation* (New York: Coward, McCann & Geoghegan, 1980) when I first read it, and later readings did not change that impression one bit. His book was a great help to me in thinking about and writing mine.

INTRODUCTION

An outline of the stages of life, as Gail Sheehy defines them, begins on page 37 in *Passages: Predictable Crises of Adult Life* (New York: Bantam Books, 1977). Information about the "urge to merge" begins on page 92, and the quote about brownies is on page 155. Sheehy's remarks about generation and the life cycle are on page 33, and those about the upcoming generation appear on page 294. (Also on that page, Sheehy correctly predicts the rush of baby-boom women to have children once they reached thirty.) Wendy's comment is on page 164 and Peter's on page 144 of J. M. Barrie's *Peter Pan* (New York: Bantam, 1985). Gail Sheehy's newer book is called *The Spirit of Survival* (New York: William Morrow & Co., Inc., 1986). The passage from Lippmann comes from his *A Preface to Morals* (New York: The Macmillan Co., 1929), page 183.

1. CREDENTIALS

I found the outline of Havighurst's developmental formula in *The Hearts of Men*, page 18, and Gould's words about early adulthood in *Transformations: Growth and Change in Adult Life* (New York: Touchstone, 1979), page 71 (the beginning of the chapter that also offers options for those aged twenty-two to twenty-eight). William James's thoughts about the self appear on page 125 of *The Philosophy of William James*, selected from his chief works, with an introduction, by Horace M. Kallen (New York: The Modern Library, 1953); the "self of selves" appears on page 139; the following passages from James can be found on pages 143, 145, and 234 respectively.

Housing costs vary across the country, of course, but a "starter" Levittown house in 1985 cost $90,000, according to Phillip Longman's editorial, "The Downwardly Mobile Baby Boomers," published in *The Wall Street Journal* on February 12, 1985. The increased percentage of college graduates is cited in *The Postponed Generation: Why American Youth Are Growing Up Later*, by Susan Littwin (New York: William Morrow & Co., Inc., 1986), page 28. The information about taxi drivers comes from a page-one article, "For Many Cabbies Today, It's Not Noo Yawk" by Maureen Dowd, *The New York Times*, January 23, 1986. Demographers' reports on if and when we marry, divorce, have children, etc., are constantly revised, updated, and sensationalized; I've tried not to be hysterical myself about rereporting these. A calm summary of recent statistics appears in "Snapshot of a Changing America," *Time*, September 2, 1985, pages 16–19.

2. INVENTING ADULTHOOD

My example of the tailor in seventeenth-century England is adapted from a similar example of a baker in *The World We*

Have Lost. Other information about man's changing ideas about himself come from *The Past and the Present* and general reading elsewhere.

3. FALSE STANDARDS

That the baby-boom generation began to turn forty in 1986 was big news that year, and the quote comes from *Time*'s cover story, May 19, 1986, page 23. Much of the background information about the fifties in this chapter comes from Eric F. Goldman's *The Crucial Decade—and After: America, 1945–1960* (New York: Vintage Books, 1960); the quote beginning, "No matter the rampant boom," appears there on page 265. Nearly all the statistics pertaining to the parents of the baby-boom generation—fertility, age of marriage, etc.— in this chapter come from *Great Expectations,* pages 19–35 and *The American People: A Timely Exploration of a Changing America and the Important New Demographic Trends Around Us* by Bryant Robey (New York: Truman Talley Books/E. P. Dutton, 1985), pages 15–50. Although these statistics (always subject to a few give-and-take percentage points) turn up in many other books, the authors presented them unusually clearly within the context of the postwar generation. I found useful information about the G.I. Bill, home ownership, and highways in *Redesigning the American Dream: The Future of Housing, Work, and Family Life* by Dolores Hayden (New York and London: W. W. Norton & Co., 1984), pages 6–12. Jacques's influential article appears in Issue 46, and is best set in context in *Surviving Middle Age* by Mike Hepworth and Mike Featherstone (Oxford: Basil Blackwell Publisher Ltd., 1982), page 42. Maureen Howard's comment appears in *Facts of Life* (New York and Harmondsworth, England: Penguin Books, 1980), page 75. The dates that "normal family life went off the air" are available in *Boom: Talkin' 'Bout Our Generation* by Joel Makower (Chicago: A Tilden Press Book/Contemporary Books, Inc., 1985), page 119. Ehrenreich's observation about maturity appears in *The Hearts of Men,* page 88.

4. SOME CHILDHOODS

The quote from *Private Lives: Men and Women of the Fifties* by Benita Eisler (New York, London, Toronto, Sydney: Franklin Watts, 1986) is taken from page 187. *The Lonely Crowd: A Study of the Changing American Character* by David Riesman, in collaboration with Reuel Denney and Nathan Glazer (New Haven: Yale University Press, 1950) was indispensable background reading for this chapter; the references cited appear on pages 9, 14, and 42 respectively. Levittown is described in *Redesigning the American Dream,* page 6; Levitt's quote about communism appears on page 8. The rise of the suburbs is documented on pages 12 and 13, and also in *Great Expectations,* pages 38–40. The figures comparing education by generation are also in *Great Expectations,* page 87. The size and spacing of families are discussed in *The Rites of Passage,* page 115.

5. A QUESTION OF BALANCE

I found Abbie Hoffman's famous quote in *Boom,* page 274. Kurt Vonnegut's quote from *Galápagos* (New York: Delacorte Press, 1986), is found on page 122. Information about the changing numbers of kids in college is from *The Postponed Generation,* pages 28 and 29, and *Great Expectations,* page 87. The "off we skip" passage from *Peter Pan* appears on page 106. Sales figures for *The Greening of America* came from R. R. Bowker, and Yeats's lines are from his collection *Responsibilities and Other Poems* (New York: The Macmillan Co., 1916), page 115.

6. CALLING CARD

Whyte's chapter "The Well-Rounded Man" in *The Organization Man* (Garden City, New York: Doubleday/Anchor Books, 1957) offers a clear profile of the fifties organization man; the first two quotes are, in order, on pages 144 and

143, and the company president's comment appears on page 150. The questions Goodman poses are in the preface to *Growing Up Absurd* (New York: Vintage Books, 1960), page xiv. Ehrenreich's chapter on *Playboy* begins on page 42; her discussion of Type-A behavior begins on page 81. The particular study on the downtrend in income cited is from *America in Perspective: Major Trends in the United States Through the 1990s, Oxford Analytica* (Boston: Houghton Mifflin, 1986); the quote is taken from page 59. Overqualified college students are discussed throughout *The Postponed Generation;* the statistic noted here appears on page 28. This book is also the source for the "theory" that it now takes an extra decade to grow up, page 245.

7. IDENTITY

"Identity formation" is discussed in *Transformations*, page 67. The comment on self-discovery through others can be found in *Habits of the Heart*, page 84. Ernest G. Schachtel's essay is called "On Alienated Concepts of Identity" and is anthologized in *Man Alone: Alienation in Modern Society,* edited, with an introduction, by Eric and Mary Josephson (New York: Dell/A Laurel Edition, 1968); the quotes appear there on pages 74 and 83. I found Jung's essay "The Stages of Life" in *Modern Man in Search of a Soul,* translated by W. S. Dell and Cary F. Baynes (San Diego, New York, London: A Harvest/HBJ Book, first published in 1933); the quote appears on page 109. Russell's thoughts about happiness are from *The Conquest of Happiness* (New York: Liveright, 1971), pages 16 and 17.

8. ALONE

The excerpt from Anne Tyler's *The Clock Winder* (New York: Berkley Books, 1983) appears on page 107. Statistics on living alone were taken from *The American People*, page 40. The change in the "sphere of individual decision" is noted in *Habits of the Heart,* page 89. The curious information about household size in Manhattan and the leper colony comes from *The American People,* page 36. *Transformations* covers the single life in fewer than ten lines, on page 120. Peter Townsend's essay on isolation and loneliness is included in *Man Alone;* the extract appears on page 326. I found Lewis's remarks on loneliness in *A Mind Awake: An Anthology of C. S. Lewis,* edited by Clyde S. Kilby (San Diego, New York, London: A Harvest/HBJ Book, 1968), page 24. "Self-Reliance" appears in *Essays by Ralph Waldo Emerson,* with an introduction by Irwin Edman (New York: Thomas Y. Crowell Co., Apollo Edition, 1961). The short passages I've chosen appear on pages 36, 49, 38, 39, 62, and 52 respectively.

9. KINSHIP

The changing concepts of "family" are well summarized in *The World We Have Lost;* the specific passage in *Home: A Short History of an Idea* by Witold Rybczynski (New York: Viking, 1986) appears on page 28. *The Social Contract: A Personal Inquiry into the Evolutionary Sources of Order and Disorder* by Robert Ardrey (New York: Atheneum, 1970) is about our needs for various kinds of attachments; the quote here is from page 81. Lillian B. Rubin backs up Ardrey in *Just Friends: The Role of Friendship in Our Lives* (New York: Harper & Row, 1985), page 22. The information on household size comes from *The American People,* page 37, and is widely available elsewhere. Rubin's second quote appears on page 4; the information about the Iroquois comes from *Kinship and Marriage: An Anthropological Perspective* by Robin Fox (Harmondsworth, England: Penguin Books, 1967), page 19. *The Wall Street Journal* article referred to appears in the edition of September 22, 1986, section 2, page 1.

10. MEN, WOMEN, EQUALITY, AND LOVE

Letty Cottin Pogrebin refers to the study of marriage, happiness, and health in *Family Politics: Love and Power on an Intimate Front* (New York: McGraw-Hill Book Co., 1984), page 87. Infidelity rates among postwar philanderers are estimated in Maggie Scarf's "Intimate Partners," *The Atlantic Monthly*, November 1986, page 47. When *Life Begins at Forty* (New York: Whittlesey House/McGraw-Hill, 1932) was published, the life expectancy in this country was fifty-five years. Goodman's quote appears on page 13, and Goffman's on page 133. Alice S. Rossi's "Sex and Gender in the Aging Society" appears in *Our Aging Society: Paradox and Promise*, edited by Alan Pifer and Lydia Bronte (New York and London: W. W. Norton & Co., 1986), page 132.

11. MARRIAGE

That a notice announcing each marriage was posted in colonial New England is mentioned in my earlier book, *Honorable Intentions: The Manners of Courtship in the '80s* (New York: Atheneum, 1983), page 20. Outside institutions replacing the family are discussed in *The Past and the Present*, page 222. Marriage as a source of psychological gratification is redefined in *Habits of the Heart*, beginning on page 85, from which the quote here is drawn. I've quoted the comments of the man who married in the fifties from *Private Lives*, page 203. Mary Borden sets forth the "bitter truth" about marriage in *The Technique of Marriage* (Garden City, New York: Doubleday, Doran & Co., 1933), page 300.

12. MAINTENANCE OF THE WORLD

Ernest Becker presents his "paradox" in *The Denial of Death* (New York: The Free Press/Macmillan, 1973) on page 173, as well as his mention of the gift "society specifies in advance." Erik H. Erikson's first qualifier about generativity is from his *Identity and the Life Cycle* (New York: W. W. Norton & Co., 1959), page 103, and the "maintenance of the world" passage is from his *Dimensions of a New Identity: The Jefferson Lectures in the Humanities* (New York: W. W. Norton & Co., 1974), page 124.

13. THE CYCLE

Lippmann's observation about childhood appears in *A Preface to Morals,* page 191, and his direct quote appears in the same volume, page 184. The age at which the mid-life crisis takes place has variously been set by Gail Sheehy, George Vaillant, Daniel Levinson, and Jane Fonda, among others. The changing median age of our society comes from *The Rites of Passage,* page 38. I've taken Henry James's wry comment about aging from David P. Barash's witty *Aging: An Exploration* (Seattle and London: University of Seattle Press, 1983), page 5. V. S. Pritchett's words on aging are from his essay "As Old as the Century" in *The Turn of the Years* (New York: Random House, 1982), pages 33 and 44 respectively.

SELECTED ADDITIONAL READING

Allen, Frederick Lewis. *Since Yesterday: The 1930s in America.* New York: Perennial Library, 1972.

Crew, Peter. *The Inner World of the Middle-Aged Man.* New York: Macmillan Publishing Co., Inc., 1976.

Dubos, René. *So Human an Animal.* New York: Charles Scribner's Sons, 1968.

Erikson, Erik H. *Childhood and Society,* 2nd ed., revised and enlarged. New York and London, W. W. Norton & Co., 1978.

————. *The Life Cycle Completed: A Review.* New York and London: W. W. Norton & Co., 1985.

Fisher, David Hackett. *Growing Old in America: The Bland-Lee Lectures Delivered at Clark University.* New York: Oxford University Press, 1977.

Fried, Martha Nemes, and Morton H. Fried. *Transitions: Four Rituals in Eight Cultures.* New York: Penguin Books, 1981.

Fromm, Erich. *The Sane Society.* New York: Ballantine Books/A Fawcett Premier Book, 1983.

Hewlitt, Sylvia A. *A Lesser Life: The Myth of Women's Liberation in America.* New York: William Morrow & Co., Inc., 1986.

Hollingworth, H. L. *Mental Growth and Decline: A Survey of Developmental Psychology.* New York: D. Appleton & Co., 1927.

Levinson, Daniel J. *The Seasons of a Man's Life.* New York: Ballantine Books, 1978.

Melamed, Elissa. *Mirror, Mirror: The Terror of Not Being Young.* New York: Linden Press/Simon & Schuster, 1983.

Packard, Vance. *A Nation of Strangers.* New York: Pocket Books, 1974.

Parker, Richard. Foreword to *The Myth of the Middle Class: Notes on Affluence and Equality,* by G. William Domhoff. New York: Harper Colophon, 1972.

Reik, Theodore. *Curiosities of the Self: Illusions We Have About Ourselves.* New York: Farrar, Straus & Giroux, 1965.

Rubin, Lillian B. *Intimate Strangers: Men and Women Together.* New York: Harper Colophon, 1984.

Secunda, Victoria. *By Youth Possessed: The Denial of Age in America.* Indianapolis and New York: Bobbs-Merrill, 1984.

Simon, Anne W. *The New Years: A New Middle Age.* New York: Alfred A. Knopf, 1968.

Vaillant, George E. *Adaptation to Life.* Boston and Toronto: Little, Brown & Co., 1977.

INDEX